Evangelical Theories of Biblical Inspiration

A REVIEW AND PROPOSAL

Kern Robert Trembath

New York   Oxford
OXFORD UNIVERSITY PRESS
1987

Oxford University Press

Oxford   New York   Toronto
Delhi   Bombay   Calcutta   Madras   Karachi
Petaling Jaya   Singapore   Hong Kong   Tokyo
Nairobi   Dar es Salaam   Cape Town
Melbourne   Auckland

and associated companies in
Beirut   Berlin   Ibadan   Nicosia

Library of Congress Cataloging-in-Publication Data

Trembath, Kern Robert.
Evangelical theories of biblical inspiration.

Based on author's thesis (doctoral)—University of Notre Dame.
Bibliography: p.
Includes index.
1. Bible—Inspiration—History of doctrines—19th
century.   2. Bible—Inspiration—History of doctrines—
20th century.   3. Bible—Inspiration.   4. Evangelicalism—United States—History—19th century.   5. Evangelicalism—United States—History—20th century.   6. Theology, Doctrinal—United States—History—19th century.
7. Theology, Doctrinal—United States—History—20th
century.   I. Title.
BS480.T69   1987   220.1'3'0973   87-11301
ISBN 0-19-504911-X

2 4 6 8 9 7 5 3 1
Printed in the United States of America
on acid-free paper

To Philip Wayne Trembath, the past,
who began in me the process of faith seeking understanding,
and
To Mark Philip Trembath, the future,
in whom God's grace so happily resides.

Acknowledgments

This work began as a doctoral dissertation at the University of Notre Dame. Even more than most books, therefore, it reflects the influence of many colleagues and friends. Perhaps this is only fitting for a book on inspiration. Foremost among the colleagues are those who sat with patient and imaginative oversight on my dissertation board: Fr. David Burrell, C.S.C., Dr. Nathan Hatch, and Fr. Robert Krieg, C.S.C. In addition, several graduate students risked many hours of their lives to encourage me to think more rigorously as both an evangelical and a critical theologian: David Hunter, Sr. Theresa Koernke, I.H.M., Edward Laarman, Gerard Paré, Charles Pinches, and Judith Sanderson. A word of sincere and heartfelt thanks is gratefully expressed to the Department of Theology of Notre Dame, and especially to Fr. Richard McBrien and Dr. F. Ellen Weaver, who have gone far out of their way both to teach me and to employ me in my attempt to make the transition from student to teacher. William Abraham, on whose shoulders much of the structure of this work rests, was comprehensive in his review and criticism of one of the prepublication drafts, and it is doubly stronger because of him. Finally, in this age of word processors it is usually the case that one will do one's own manuscript preparation, but I would be remiss were I to overlook all of the time, counsel, and resources which the Notre Dame Computing Center literally donated to me.

Among those whose contribution was less academic but not less real, I am especially indebted to my families. My brother, Rev. Raymond Trembath, contributed many insightful comments about the work. Patricia Haag gave me large doses of encouragement during the year it took to write it. And my parents, Harry and Caroline Trembath, have been nothing less than saints in supporting my interminable graduate education. This is a small first step in what I hope is a long career whose foundation was provided by them.

Finally, how does one adequately express thanks to a dissertation director? Fr. James T. Burtchaell, C.S.C., saw far earlier than I the possibilities and the outline of the work which this eventually became, and thus its strengths are mostly his while its weaknesses are entirely mine. His theological insights are explicitly mentioned only a few times in the pages which follow, but they reside between the lines of nearly every one of them. The value of his contribution is exceeded only by the degree to which he let me work on my own, and his grace as a person, as a theologian, and as a writer will never leave me. I can only hope that other dissertationists enjoy their directors as much as I did mine.

There are a few places where the material herein overlaps with some that I have published elsewhere. I would like to acknowledge the permission to republish these materials which was generously extended by *The Evangelical Quarterly* ("Biblical Inspiration and the Believing Community: A New Look," vol. 58, no. 3 (July 1986), pp. 245–56); and *Horizons: The Journal of the College Theological Society* ("Was the Incarnation Redundant? A Catholic and an Evangelical Respond," vol. 13, no. 1 (1986), pp. 43–66). Bible quotations have been taken from the Revised Standard Version of the Bible, ©1946, 1952, and 1971, by the Division of Christian Education of the National Council of the Churches of Christ in the United States of America, and are used by permission.

Contents

Introduction	**3**
1. Deductivist Theories of Biblical Inspiration	**8**
Charles Hodge	10
Benjamin Breckenridge Warfield	20
John Warwick Montgomery	27
Edward John Carnell	37
Conclusion	45
2. Inductivist Theories of Biblical Inspiration	**47**
Augustus H. Strong	48
Bernard Ramm	57
William J. Abraham	64
Conclusion	70
3. Inspiration and the Human Recipient	**72**
Interest in Methodology	72
Basic Anthropology	75
The Activity of the Mind and Biblical Inspiration	81
Conclusion	86
4. Inspiration and the Means	**87**
The Verbal Inspiration of the Bible	88
The Plenary Inspiration of the Bible	92

The Inerrancy of the Bible   96
Conclusion   103

5. God as the Initiator of Inspiration   **104**

The Transcendental Theology of Karl Rahner   105
Divine Inspiration and Biblical Inspiration   109
A Concluding Comment   114

Notes   **119**

Bibliography   **143**

Index   **151**

Evangelical Theories of Biblical Inspiration

Introduction

The past decade has seen an energetic resurgence of books and articles by Protestants on the subject of biblical inspiration. For many prior decades the topic lay dormant, a condition fostered by naïveté and neglect from church "conservatives" and outright dismissal from church "liberals." The current renascence of interest in inspiration may thus be seen as a judgment by both wings of the church upon their former ways of treating the subject, a judgment which, like all honest reappraisals, carries with it the potential of significant advances in theological understanding. As such, there is reason enough to justify the effort.

There exists, though, another and perhaps more positive reason why this subject deserves greater attention within the church. Father James T. Burtchaell notes in his *Catholic Theories of Biblical Inspiration since 1810* that "the controversy over biblical inspiration is an excellent test case whereby to diagnose many of the ills that have weakened Catholic theology, especially since the Reformation. The real issue here is what confounds scholars in so many areas: the manner in which individual human events are jointly caused by both God and man." He then goes on to suggest that "today the most easily examined instance of divine-human responsibility is the Bible."[1]

This diagnosis and suggested therapy is one with which I heartily agree, not just for Catholics but for Orthodox and Protestants as well. The topic of inspiration gives theologians the opportunity to conjoin many discrete fields of inquiry: theology proper (the doctrine of God), theological anthropology (Christian reflection upon human beings), biblical exegesis (the science of text criticism and hermeneutics), and ecclesiology (the doctrine of the church). Inspiration thus calls for specialists in each of these fields to expand their horizons to the others, for at this conjunction, as at few others, nearsightedness guarantees superficiality.

This book is written from within a particular segment of the church—American evangelicalism—although it is addressed to both those who would and those who would not choose to describe themselves as evangelicals. Thus we need to define evangelicalism, however briefly, in order to account for our selection of inspiration theorists. There are three broad criteria or principles which, in our opinion, constitute the meaning of evangelicalism. The first two are the traditional "formal and material principles" of Protestantism and are accepted by nearly all as constitutive of evangelicalism.[2] The formal principle recognizes the critical priority of the Bible for all of Christian life and reflection; according to the ancient dictum, the Bible is the standard of last appeal (*norma normans sed non normata*). Evangelicalism thus accepts the priority but not the exclusivity of the Bible in religious matters; the dictum does not claim that the Bible is the only guide, but simply that it is the ultimate guide, for the church.

The material principle of Protestantism further specifies the first one by confessing that Jesus of Nazareth was, and is, God's sign of reconciliation with the world. Because Jesus appeared empirically to be like all other persons of his time, this confession concerning him is not a simple historical observation. Rather, it is a confession of faith; it is a confession that in Jesus the world has been reconciled to God and has thus been empowered to live a life which reflects both the freedom and the responsibility of living as a community of believers.

The third principle of evangelicalism is less traditional than the first two. It is that evangelicalism is constitutively transdenominational or pluralistic in nature. Of the three great branches of Christianity, only Protestantism has chosen to create new structures each time differences have surfaced from within. This habit varies not only from the ways that Catholics and Orthodox treat diversity, but it varies as well from how the first-century church handled diversity within itself, as James D. G. Dunn has shown in his *Unity and Diversity in the New Testament*.[3] Evangelicals, however, proceed differently from other Protestants. In defining as "evangelical" members of a great range of denominations, evangelicalism discloses a greater implicit emphasis upon the experience of salvation in Jesus than upon cognitive, dogmatic, and historical articulations of this experience. Such articulations are not valueless altogether but are simply of less value than they are to a nonevangelical or "denominational" mindset. Thus, considered ecclesiologically, evangelicalism is Protestantism's clearest attempt to recapture the pluralistic nature of the early church. I do not claim that this has always been a deliberate attempt but only that it is the way that some Protestants seek to bless, rather than curse, theological diversity.

The critical significance of this third principle is that this book will not survey those theologians whose ecclesiologies are deliberately exclusive or sectarian in nature. Such ecclesiologies cannot adequately account for the spectrum of alternative and legitimate forms of Christian belief and activity present within the canonical Scriptures. I will instead consider those theologians whose works were directed toward, and accepted by, many Christian communities. Likewise, I shall feel free to draw upon theologians from a variety of backgrounds.

This book proceeds in the two stages implicit in its subtitle. The first two chapters involve a review of representative inspiration theories. Chapter 1 surveys deductivist theories. I will further define deductivism below, but it may be stated in general that such theories begin with the element of the divine in biblical inspiration rather than the human. Chapter 2 takes up inductivist theories, which generally attempt to balance the divine and human agencies in the inspiration of the Bible. For this reason, they have greater potential for accounting for the "joint causation" of the Bible referred to above. In particular, the inductivist approach calls attention to the fact that analysis of the concept of inspiration best begins by inspecting those communities which claim to be inspired; only then does it work "backwards" to consider the initiator and the means of inspiration.

The second part of the book is my proposal for how biblical inspiration ought to be understood. Chapters 3 through 5 consider the recipients of inspiration (human beings), the medium of inspiration (the Bible), and the initiator of inspiration (God). Here we shall discover that the traditional evangelical understanding of anthropology leads to the conclusion that people cannot learn *about* God except by learning *from* God. From this we can see that a particular means of learning about God need not possess extraordinary, miraculous, or "divine" characteristics in order to be a vehicle for knowledge of God. Rather, the initial critical question to ask is whether that means of learning is consonant with salvation as experienced and understood by the Christian community. I shall thus propose that "the inspiration of the Bible" should be taken to refer not to empirical characteristics of the Bible itself but rather to the fact that the church confesses the Bible as God's primary means of inspiring salvation within itself. Finally, I shall suggest that the doctrine of God which best coordinates with inspiration understood in this way is that offered by Karl Rahner and other so-called transcendentalists.

A final note: The verse that has traditionally been interpreted as the Bible's only reference to itself as "inspired" is 2 Timothy 3:16: "All Scripture is *theopneustos* . . . ," or, "All *theopneustos* Scripture. . . ." Most treatises on biblical inspiration, especially those from the more conservative wings of the church, spend careful time in examining the concept of *theopneustos*. This one does not; in fact, the only time I mention the word is in my consideration of B. B. Warfield's use of it.

The reason for this is twofold. First, two kinds of assumptions must be made in order to warrant the use of *theopneustos* in inspiration discussions. The first assumption is that we know what the word means, but we do not, in spite of the staggering amount of attention it has received over several generations. *Theopneustos* is a *hapax legomenon:* it occurs only here in the Bible, and only rarely outside it. Thus we have extremely little to go on in order to discover what the author of 2 Timothy intended by the word, and not nearly enough to justify its use as a critical factor in inspiration discussions.

The second assumption, contingent on the first, is that we know which Scriptures the author meant to call *theopneustos,* as distinct from those which were not. Were they the present Old Testament canon? In Hebrew or in Greek? Oral or written? Including or excluding the Apocrypha? The "auto-graphs" or the manuscripts available to the author in the first century? The answers to each of these questions would give a different meaning to *theopneustos,* but since we have no way of knowing the answers, we have no indisputable way of defining the word. Thus, it cannot serve to inform our present deliberations concerning inspiration.

The second reason why I choose not to consider *theopneustos* is of another kind altogether and requires the introduction of a technical distinction. Let us distinguish between "Bible" and "Scripture," with the former referring to the collection of sixty-six books called by that name and the latter referring to the way the church receives those books, that is, as religiously normative. According to this understanding, any material which is called Scripture is so called because it is taken as religiously authoritative. For Jews and Christians (at least), this means that the material is seen ultimately as "coming from God," however that "coming from" is explained. In a very important sense, to confess that "Scripture is inspired by God" is a tautology, because that statement *means* that "the material which comes from God comes from God." As Paul Achtemeier has shown in his *The Inspiration of Scripture,* not even today's liberals believe that the inspiration of the Bible is utterly identical with aesthetic inspiration (although many of their nineteenth-century forebears did). Rather, today almost all would agree that biblical inspiration is a special kind of inspiration; the task of interested people then becomes to define what is special about it.

The point I wish to make, though, is that the specific difference between perceiving the book as "Bible" and perceiving it as "Scripture" has to do with salvation. It is the presence or absence of salvation which differentiates between reading the book as Scripture or reading it only as Bible. So one way to describe my purpose in this book is to discuss how it is that the Bible becomes Scripture for the believing community, that is, how a particular collection of books serves as the ultimate means through which God awakens salvation within the community that is then called the church. That is why I have written about biblical, rather than scriptural, inspiration; I wished from the outset to emphasize that the presence (or absence) of salvation is utterly crucial in discussing the meaning of inspiration. The book called the Bible is read very differently by nonbelievers and believers, and whatever accounts for this difference is central to the notion of inspiration. I trust that what follows will prove to be a helpful contribution to the church's understanding of itself as the community inspired to salvation by the Father of Jesus through the Bible.

1

Deductivist Theories
of Biblical Inspiration

In this chapter I shall examine four theories of biblical inspiration. They are related by a common method or approach, which may be called a deductivist approach. A deductivist approach is one that reflects the understanding that knowledge is grounded upon beliefs which are not subject to empirical verification but nevertheless guide or influence empirical observations. Such beliefs are often uncritically held; persons holding them assume them without examining them. In addition, and probably because they are never critically inspected, these beliefs are taken to be inviolable. They therefore shape and influence major portions of mental and empirical activity but remain impervious to influence themselves. Since such beliefs logically antedate all mental and empirical activity according to this approach, it is also referred to as an a priori scheme of knowledge. I shall use these two terms interchangeably.

In general, deductivist approaches to biblical inspiration begin by discussing and formulating a doctrine of God. Since a part of any doctrine of God is that God cannot lie or deceive, anything said to be "the word of God" must (*ex hypothesi*) be the truth. The Bible has been called the word of God, and thus it too has been taken to be "the truth." A deductivist theory of biblical inspiration must explain how the books of the Bible, which at least appear to be like many other books, can be called the word of God in such a way that their complete truthfulness is ensured. The genius of a deductivist approach to inspiration lies in its confession of the cause-and-effect relationship between the character of God and the truthfulness of the Bible. This is what William Abraham means when he says, "A deductive type of theory begins with a basic theological claim about the meaning of inspiration and attempts to deduce from this what Scripture must be or contain."[1] The a priori element in this approach is the content of both the doctrine of God and the doctrine of inspiration, which is determined independent of any human experiential consideration, especially any critical or reflective experience with the text of the Bible.

The four authors I shall survey are united in their belief that they are upholding the clear teaching of the Bible, as well as the "evangelical" core of church teaching, concerning inspiration. It was not their intention to add distinctively new elements to the inspiration question but rather simply to develop what was latent within it. We shall see, however, that their intentions were contradicted by their accomplishments, perhaps inevitably. Given their historical context, especially with respect to developments in geology and biblical criticism, it seems unreasonable to expect them to have defended the traditional doctrine of inspiration without reference to that context or without responding to those new developments. If theology is to be more than regurgitatively historical on the one hand or faddishly reactionary on the other, it must always seek to relate the new with the old. The problem with the evangelicals we shall study here is not so much that they did not recognize that they were adding to the doctrine of inspiration, that is, with "the new." It is rather with "the old," that which they took to be "biblical" and thus in need of defense. We shall see that they read the Bible through interpretive grids which were neither faithful to the biblical texts nor critically evaluated, and which are seen to be deficient when scrutinized.

All four theories are species within the same genus, but they are hardly identical. In fact, they have been selected because of the variety of ways in which they exemplify the deductivist method. Charles Hodge and Benjamin B. Warfield share the greatest number of denominational and conceptual similarities. They are the major figures in the so-called Princeton school of theology, a school of thought characterized by analysis of the Bible conducted logically by means of premises and principles discovered in the Bible. However, Hodge and Warfield did not at all see eye to eye on, for example, the degree to which modern science, especially geology, may properly inform the interpretation of the Bible. John Warwick Montgomery presents a deductivist historiography according to which the truth of the Bible is inferred from the historical accuracy of the gospel authors in recording the life of Jesus. Finally, the early Edward John Carnell understands inspiration as that which accounts for the "systematic consistency" of the Bible. For him, the truth of the Bible rests on the fact that it is God's rendition of both logic and history.

In general, I shall bring two questions to bear on each of the theories discussed. First, did the authors follow an inductivist methodology, as they claimed, or were they actually influenced by uninspected premises and assumptions that guaranteed certain kinds of conclusions about the Bible? Second, were their doctrines concerning the Bible taken from the Bible itself, or were they drawn instead from what the church believed about the Bible? With respect to both pairs of questions, my contention will be that these evangelicals asserted the former but practiced the latter.

I am not unsympathetic to the concern of the authors to articulate a defensible theory of biblical inspiration. Indeed, at all times my criticisms are offered with the intention of articulating just such a theory. For this reason, I hope that the reader whose own understanding of inspiration is represented here may feel challenged "from within" and thus feel the need, or at least the curiosity, to consider the theory of biblical inspiration which this book proposes.

Charles Hodge

"In every science there are two factors: facts and ideas; or, facts and the mind." Thus begins the three-volume *Systematic Theology* of Charles Hodge (1797–1878), a man recognized within Reformed Protestantism as "one of the greatest Reformed theologians."[2] All scientific activity operates, he explains, by collecting raw or given data and relating them so that their "harmony and consistency" are demonstrated.[3] Genuine scientific activity is more than simple observation of the given. It is also the deliberate arrangement of the given so that their internal relations ("laws of nature") may be exhibited and ascertained. Only in this way may the goal of science—greater knowledge of the past and predictive ability over the future—be achieved.

Theology is also a science and thus operates inductively as do the natural sciences. Its method is likewise to argue from effect to cause, to "begin with collecting well-established facts, and from them infer the general laws which determine their occurrence."[4] The theologian resembles the natural scientist in at least three ways. First, the assumptions they make are similar. Both must assume the trustworthiness of sense perceptions, of cognitive reliability, and of those truths which are not themselves facts but are implicit in the recognition and acquisition of facts (e.g., cause and effect). Second, both must respect the objectivity of the data with which they work. Facts must be neither manufactured nor modified. Third, both deduce operative laws from their observational activity. Some account must be made of the pattern and regularity observed by careful and consistent attention to the data. As over against Kant, Hodge insists that these laws "are not derived from the mind, and attributed to external objects, but [are rather] derived or deduced from the objects and impressed upon the mind."[5]

For the natural scientist, nature is the locus of the facts to be interrelated inductively. For the theologian, that locus is the Bible. The Bible is the storehouse in which are situated "all the facts which God has revealed concerning Himself and our relation to Him."[6] Scripture is not only the source of theological data, however. It is also that which ultimately evaluates that data. Thus it stands as locus of facts needing to be interpreted but also as superfact doing the very act of interpretation and not itself in need of interpretation.

This significant deviation from the status of "natural" facts is admitted when Hodge notes that "theological" facts are found in the Bible but also in creation, in human nature, and in religious experience. Only the Bible, however, is finally able to adjudicate and authenticate true from false religious inductions.[7] This distinction is consistent with the traditional formal principle of Protestantism (*sola Scriptura*). What is unexpected is that it is introduced without fanfare or apology in a treatise whose intent is to demonstrate the methodological identity of the natural and the theological enterprises. This "dialectical" relationship between facts as objective data and facts as critical data is much more representative of contemporary pragmatic theory of science than it was of the induction of Hodge's day.[8] One has the feeling that Hodge was not so much prescient as he was faithful to *sola Scriptura,* a fidelity which in this instance illustrates the cultural tension in which many evangelical theologians found themselves in the nineteenth century. Hodge's fidelity to *sola Scriptura* did not, however, prevent him from attempting to integrate it into a larger method of inquiry which was at odds with it: the inductivist method. He did not suffer from a failure of nerve.

We may now account for including Hodge's inductive methodology within the discussion of deductivist approaches to biblical inspiration. The reason is straightforward: Hodge exempted the Bible itself from the corpus of data needing inductive analysis. The Bible, for Hodge, is the ultimate interpretive check on all theological activity because it alone contains "the facts" unalloyed by human subjectivity. The task of the systematic theologian is to arrange and exhibit the facts given by God and collected in the Bible so as to show their internal relation to each other. These "internal relations" are to theological facts what "theory" is to the facts of nature, and it is "the fundamental principle of all sciences, and of theology among the rest, that theory is to be determined by facts, and not facts by theory."[9] "The Bible contains all the facts or truths which form the contents of theology, just as the facts of nature are the contents of the natural sciences."[10]

This is the very assumption against which uncritical or simple inductivism later stumbled and fell: that facts are simply what the senses and the mind say they are. Hodge believed that facts do not need interpretation so much as they provide the foundation for it. Biblical facts are concrete and God-given, and their relations with each other are "in" them. The task of the theologian is therefore simply to extricate and illuminate these relations, not to inspect the attitude which sees the facts themselves as irreducibly foundational.

If there is a criticism of Hodge here, it is not the facile one that he was inconsistent in his use of the inductive model. Rather, it is that he failed to recognize the similarity between the mind's apprehending "facts" and the mind's apprehending "relations or theories." In neither case is the mind completely passive, as Hodge supposed with respect to the apprehension of facts. In neither case may it be said that a given datum is beyond the need for critical interpretation. In placing biblical data beyond that need, Hodge thereby precluded them from constituting genuine objects of knowledge as well.

Hodge's "inductive" methodology is evident in his treatise on inspiration, to which I now turn. (That the treatise itself is located in the introduction to the work as a whole further supports my claim that Hodge is in actuality a deductive theologian.) It will be seen that Hodge grounds his discussion of inspiration variously on three types of foundations: a bare or simple appeal to the Bible as the Word of God (the Bible thus possessing the authority of its primary author), an appeal to both sacred and profane antiquity, and an appeal to natural theology. As noted earlier, that there are both a priori and a posteriori elements in Hodge's approach should probably be taken as evidence not of his confusion or indecision, but of his openness to epistemological advances[11] at odds with the Protestant scholasticism which he and his evangelical contemporaries had inherited.[12]

Hodge begins by noting the unanimity of Protestant confessions that the Scriptures are the only infallible rule of faith and practice.[13] This is "due to the fact that they are the word of God; and they are the word of God because they were given by inspiration of the Holy Ghost."[14] Thus, as prolegomenon even to the systematic analysis of the doctrine of God, quite apart from his analysis of anthropology, Hodge presents a distinct morphology of the God-human relationship. God exists independently of His creation. He is "extra-mundane," that is, not merely the "soul, life, or animating principle" of the universe. Further, although "[He] generally acts according to fixed laws and through secondary causes, He is free to act, and often does act immediately, without the intervention of such causes, as in creation, regeneration, and miracles."[15]

Inspiration is another such occurrence of immediate divine activity. It is "an influence of the Holy Spirit on the minds of certain select men, which rendered them the organs of God for the infallible communication of His mind and will. They were in such a sense the organs of God, that what they said God said."[16] This act of inspiration is distinct both from divine providence and from "spiritual illumination" or regeneration. It differs from providence in that it is an immediate supernatural activity; the mediation of secondary causes is not operative in the act of inspiration. It differs from spiritual illumination in three respects: the subject (a few persons rather than all true believers), the intent (securing infallibility as teachers rather than "rendering men holy"), and the effect (inspiration in itself has no sanctifying influence). The primary "object or design of inspiration is to secure infallibility in teaching."[17] It thus has to do not with the content of knowledge communicated but rather with the certainty of transferring that knowledge from primary author to written text. The significance of this (traditional) distinction between revelation and inspiration is that the origins of a particular text are irrelevant with respect to the doctrine of inspiration. "If the sacred writers have sufficient sources of knowledge in themselves, or in those about them, there is no need to assume any direct revelation. . . . No more causes are to be assumed for any effect than are necessary."[18]

Hodge substantiates this conception of inspiration from both inside and outside the Scriptures. From inside the Scriptures, Hodge cites the figure of the prophet. Because

> the law was written by Moses, and as Moses was the greatest of the prophets, it follows that all the Old Testament was written by prophets. If, therefore, we can determine the Scriptural idea of a prophet, we shall thereby determine the character of their writings and the authority due to them. [19]

A prophet speaks for another in such a way that the words and message belong to the other and not to the prophet. Moses' ordination is here cited as warrant both for his own and for Aaron's prophetic status (Ex. 4:14–16). The signs of prophecy par excellence, therefore, are the divine formulae "Behold, I have put my words in thy mouth" and "Thus saith the Lord." Peter's assertion in 2 Peter 1:20–21 confirms this with respect to the Old Testament and establishes it with respect to the New.[20]

Hodge also cites extrabiblical sources in justification of his definition. Lexical analyses of the words *theophoroi, entheos,* and *pneumatophoros* indicate to him that "All nations have entertained the belief that not only has God access to the human mind and can control its operations, but that He at times did take such possession of particular persons as to make them the organs of his communications."[21] The convergence of sacred and profane conceptions of inspiration confirms that in antiquity "inspiration" had a fixed meaning identical with the phenomenon of the Israelite prophet: a primary speaker uses a secondary agent to convey a message to an audience, with inspiration guaranteeing that what the agent conveys is what the speaker intended.

Although at first glance it might appear that inspiration attaches to the person of the agent, Hodge is careful to specify the message itself as that which is protected by the speaker's (God's) infallibility. Indeed, the agent's character is all but irrelevant in the process of inspiration. Hodge is careful to deny, however, that it is rendered irrelevant by being overruled by divine dictation.[22] "The sacred writers were not made unconscious or irrational . . . [They] were not machines." Rather, they "impressed their peculiarities on their several productions as plainly as though they were the subjects of no extraordinary influence."

Hodge uses the analogy of the sanctifying activity of the Holy Spirit in the life of the believer to illustrate this point: "There is no reason to believe that the operation of the Spirit in inspiration revealed itself any more in the consciousness of the sacred writers, than His operations in sanctification reveal themselves in the consciousness of the Christian." Other evangelical writers use the categories of superintendence and providence to account for that which Hodge simply asserts, namely, that God's use of an agent in the process of inspiration need not result in the diminution of that agent's freedom or alteration of that agent's character.

A problem with Hodge's treatment is his subsequent assertion that apart from inspiration, "a mere human report or record of a divine revelation must of necessity be not only fallible, but more or less erroneous."[23] The errorlessness of the biblical message thus cannot simply be a conjoined effort of God and person, as is the case with sanctification, for errorlessness is not a constituent of sanctification as it is of inspiration.[24] The analogy between inspiration and sanctification fails at the crucial point of accounting for discernible infallibility in such a way that human freedom to err is not actually overruled by divine activity. That freedom must in fact be overruled if the effect of inspiration, unlike that of sanctification, is discernible errorlessness.

Hodge's inconsistency here could have been resolved by recourse to alternatives which he does not take. The alternative that humans *can* write faithfully and truly about God apart from immediate intervention is denied by Hodge's understanding of the entailment of original sin, that is, "the inability of fallen man in his natural state, of himself to do anything spiritually good."[25] The alternative that humans might truly learn of God by means of a fallible mediator seems not to have occurred to him within the context of the doctrine of Scripture. Any concrete evidence of human contribution to the writing of Scripture is relegated to matters of literary style which no two authors shared, and not to matters of human moral fallibility which they all shared.

For Hodge, if perhaps not for others, the more important question concerns the extent of those writings in which inspiration is operative. Thus, he speaks of plenary inspiration, a multifaceted concept meaning variously (1) that all books of Scripture are inspired and infallible, (2) that all the contents of each book are equally inspired, and (3) that whatever a book "asserts" or "teaches" is free from error because "Scripture cannot be broken" and "God cannot deceive." Partial inspiration, therefore, which is the restriction of inspiration to any but not all of these elements, is denied as not being "the Church doctrine on this subject."[26] This is not to deny varying degrees of significance and helpfulness to different parts of the Bible. "There may be as great a difference between St. John's Gospel and the Book of Chronicles as between a man's brain and his hair," but the Spirit of God is equally present in all parts of the Bible.

The negative significance of plenary inspiration is that only the message of the writer is accorded the guarantee of divine infallibility and divine presence. Inspiration (again) has to do with the transmission of knowledge from God to writing. Thus, the biblical authors were not anachronistic in their general knowledge and understanding. With respect to all human activities outside their inscripturated teachings, "they stood on the same level as their contemporaries. They were inspired only as teachers, and when acting as the spokesmen of God."[27] This brings to mind (but from another perspective) the question raised earlier of how a prophet could be utterly contemporaneous with his or her own cultural context and still be "influenced" to predict the future in such a way that the prediction would be historically and accurately fulfilled without that prophet's mental processes being overruled. The question is asked sympathetically of Hodge; it does not ignore his distinction between inspiration and revelation. But as a "transmissive" concept, inspiration guarantees that a particular prophetic utterance (for example) will be historically and infallibly fulfilled as prophesied, and thus there cannot be too great a line of demarcation between the two categories. Words are, after all, the words of persons.

One has the feeling that an equivocation is present. When the precise definition of inspiration is at issue, it is seen to apply to the process of transmission so that content (the product of revelation, illumination, and natural cognitive activity) is properly conveyed regardless of the truth or falsity of that content. Seen in this light, inspiration has nothing other than a courier function. This impression is strengthened by Hodge's use of analogies from Greek religion; one would scarcely expect him to agree with the content of such communication even while he is bold to claim its transmissive operation as warrant for his understanding of Christian inspiration. The picture is complicated, however, once Hodge begins to give concrete biblical illustrations of inspiration. As is seen par excellence in the case of the Hebrew prophets, but also in the New Testament, it is more the content that is at issue than the process conveying that content. For example, in his section titled "The Inspiration of the Scriptures Extends to the Words," Hodge cites the following reasons in support of the claim implicit in the title: that thoughts are inseparably in words; that Christ and His Apostles argue from the very words of Scripture, illustrating their divine authority; and that the "organs of God" in the communication of His will were controlled by Him in the words which they used. "The words of the prophet were the words of God, or he could not be God's spokesman and mouth."[28]

The issue here is not simply to point out inconsistencies. It is instead whether inspiration is to be taken as a doctrine of cognitive import, susceptible therefore to cognitive analysis, or as a doctrine of purely transmissive import, susceptible to logical and historical analysis. As a theologian upon whom many evangelicals subsequently depended, Hodge is ambivalent in deciding this question. He was writing when the use of historical criticism was just beginning within Protestant orthodoxy. The acceptance of such use, I have claimed, critically distinguishes evangelicals from fundamentalists. It is to his credit that this ambivalence exists, for beginning with Hodge evangelicalism found it possible to relate traditional with developing forms of hermeneutics, such as inductivism. To make this same point from a different perspective, at a time when nearly all evangelical theologians included inspiration within their doctrine of God, Hodge attempted to introduce an anthropological significance to inspiration by removing it from his *the*ology altogether. In retrospect, it must be noted that he nevertheless continued to interpret inspiration as a constituent of the doctrine of God, to be analyzed therefore by noting the "divine" qualities of the Bible itself independent of its effects upon the believing community. But an important option was opened to conservative Protestantism by his work: the use of knowledge from outside the Bible to interpret the Bible itself.

In this analysis of Charles Hodge we must take note of his brief but subsequently controversial discussion of errors in the Bible. In only three pages he defends the position that if errors do exist they are so insignificant as to be religiously irrelevant.[29] Hodge would accept two kinds of phenomena as error: internal contradiction, and direct contradiction of historical or scientific fact known as fact by modern readers.

Regarding the first, he gladly admits to the "volumes" of discrepancies alleged against biblical consistency. Curiously, though, he does not discuss any even for the heuristic purpose of challenging and denying it. Instead he simply repeats the usual types of objections *against* alleged errors: that they are trivial since they deal only with numbers or dates; that they are only apparent and "yield to careful examination"; that they result from scribal inattentiveness; and finally that "the marvel and the miracle is that there are so few of any real importance." (Warfield will find it necessary to provide an energetic midrash on this last point.) The only thing which can account for this virtual freedom from serious error is the "hypothesis that the writers were under the guidance of the Spirit of God." The believer may admit that unaccountable difficulties (still unspecified) do exist. Surely, though, "a Christian may be allowed to tread such objections under his feet."

Concerning the second type of error—that the Bible asserts facts at odds with what is known to be true from extrabiblical sources—Hodge has a defense ready at hand. One must distinguish between a fact being believed by a sacred writer and a fact being taught by a sacred writer. Since the intent of inspiration has to do with the teachings of Scripture and not the opinions which its authors held in common with their contemporaries, though, a critic would have to show that a factual error was being *taught* in order to sustain the allegation of this type of error in the Bible.

This apologetic may look like sleight of hand. It is certainly a device whose usefulness is negligible because of its inaccessibility; after all, the only persons who could conclusively adjudicate the difference between opinion and teaching are the authors themselves, and we have no independent access to their intentions. Hodge may easily be criticized, but, as before, a more sympathetic reading is possible, and this time Hodge supplies his own example.

"Science has in many things taught the Church how to understand the Scriptures." A case in point is the interpretation of Genesis 1 with respect to various states of cosmological knowledge. When Ptolemaic theory best explained cosmological observations, the Bible was read in that light. When Ptolemy was overthrown by Copernicus, the interpretation of Genesis followed suit. Tellingly, Hodge speculates that "if geologists finally prove that [the earth] has existed for myriads of ages, it will be found that the first chapter of Genesis is in full accord with the facts, and that the last results of science are embodied on the first page of the Bible." This is a remarkable assertion from one who on the same page wrote that "theories are of men [but] facts are of God." The point of interest here is the latitude that Hodge gives to the human intellect in coming to decisions over matters of interpretation, theology, and anthropology. This is no "biblicist" speaking; where there is doubt regarding whether a biblical assertion is fact or opinion, let the human community ("science") decide: "It may cost the Church a severe struggle to give up one interpretation and adopt another, as it did in the seventeenth century, but no real evil need be apprehended."

Finally, a brief word must be said about Hodge's understanding of the theological significance of the "autographs," the documents physically inscribed or dictated by the biblical authors. His *Systematic Theology* does not address this issue as such; it is not clear whether Hodge refers to the autographs or to the earliest extant manuscripts when he speaks of the inspiration and inerrancy of "the books of Scripture." What is somewhat clearer is that the "discrepancies and difficulties" of even these manuscripts called for further theological analysis than he had been able to give in this work. In 1877, in a letter to Marcus Dods of the Glasgow Presbytery, he writes: "It is of the Bible as it came from the hands of the sacred writers . . . that this infallibility is asserted. . . . There may be errors between one part of Scripture and another, arising from errors of transcribers."[30]

The significance of this statement is the evidence it gives of Hodge's belief that the authority of the Bible rests primarily upon external evidence (i.e., the inerrancy of texts) whose validity was "scientific," that is, independent of the faith perspective of the reader or the community of faith in which that reader lived. The Westminster Confession, to which all Princeton pastors and teachers subscribed, located that authority differently: ". . . our full persuasion and assurance of the infallible truth, and divine authority thereof, is from the inward work of the Holy Spirit, bearing witness by and with the Word in our hearts."[31] The "heavenliness of the matter, the efficacy of the doctrine, the majesty of the style, [and] the consent of all the parts" all give evidence to the Bible's being the Word of God.[32] In the final analysis, however, it is not these but the divine operation of the Holy Spirit in the mind and heart of the believer that ultimately brings about the recognition of the authority of the Bible. Both alternatives agree that the Scriptures come from God, but Hodge's warrant for the believer's recognition of that divine provenance signals the presence of another apologetic. No longer is the divine status of the Bible a matter simply for Christians to affirm and, at times, to debate. Now, because of the objective inerrancy of the autographs, it is a matter to which in principle all persons ought consent.[33] Hodge himself does not explicitly draw this latter conclusion, but his inductive methodology leads to it inescapably. His successors, especially Benjamin B. Warfield, developed the possibility of the complete external verifiability of the divine authority of the Bible.[34]

Hodge claimed that his understanding of biblical inspiration was simply that which was always believed and taught by the church. Speaking of the editorial stance of the *Biblical Repertory and Princeton Review,* a journal which he founded in 1825 and edited for nearly fifty years, he writes, "No article opposed to [the system of doctrine taught in the Bible] has ever appeared in its pages. . . . It is believed to be true that an original idea in theology is not to be found in [its] pages."[35] This was a naïve view. The rising use of higher criticism in Europe and subsequently in the United States demanded an apologetic for conservative Protestantism that had never previously been required.[36] Hodge's conceptual framework for mounting this new defense was Scottish realism, or Scottish commonsense philosophy. While it is not within the purpose of this book to explicate Scottish realism,[37] its fundamental outline has already been noted. But Hodge failed to notice how far his uncritical acceptance of commonsense philosophy deviated from the traditional Augustinian and Calvinist concepts of the totality of the effects of original sin. He specifically rejects, for example, speculative methodology in theology as insufficiently empirical[38] and mystical[39] methodology as too responsive to emotions or feeling.[40] Even though he warns his reader here that "conscience is much less liable to err than reason," he does not himself heed this warning with regard to the certainty of knowledge derived by the mind from the senses and from "mental operations." Why should it be thought that these cognitive activities escape the constrictions of original sin, which Calvin had used theologically to relate *all* human faculties to God? Hodge never answers this question, almost certainly because he did not see it as one.

A second contribution made by Scottish realism to Hodge's theology affects his understanding of the inspiration of the Bible more directly. Hodge followed Thomas Reid[41] in understanding words in a way similar to what would later be called the picture theory of language. Words are directly knowable by the mind and, in addition, are direct representations of the objects to which they refer. Logically, therefore, words and sense impressions are identical in that each refers directly to objects. Those objects, in turn, are directly and with utmost certainty known by the mind. "Language is the express image and picture of human thoughts; and from the picture we may draw some certain conclusions concerning the original. . . . Now, what is common in the structure of languages, indicates an [sic] uniformity of opinion in those things upon which that structure is grounded."[42] The immediacy of word and object supported by this analysis of language warranted Hodge's certainty that the words of Scripture convey infallibly to the contemporary reader what God had put into the minds of the biblical author. As Rogers and McKim note, "To read the biblical words was to encounter the biblical thought or deed just as if [the reader] had had direct experience of it."[43] From this perspective, it is nearly impossible to overestimate the literalness with which Hodge took the phrase "The Bible is God's Word."

Inspiration as a transmissive concept thus has a double sense. On the one hand, it refers to the process by which the biblical author wrote what God intended to be written. On the other, it refers to the immediacy of the modern reader's access to those divine intentions and the certainty with which the reader could know the mind of God. Small wonder, then, that Hodge spent so little time directly considering higher criticism and the autographs. What was the need, when "the Church doctrine" of inspiration accounted so adequately for both the divinely authorized status of the biblical words and for the immediate encounter of the modern reader with their divine meaning?

We have come full circle in this analysis of Hodge's understanding of biblical inspiration, but we have not ended where we began. Hodge's treatise oscillates between a view of the Bible as a storehouse of facts whose objective truth is guaranteed by divine *auctoritas* and a view of it as a locus of uninterpreted data standing in need of the contribution of human theory, not divinely given, so that human understanding may result. He thus also oscillates between viewing inspiration as a cognitive element attaching to persons and as constituting a mere process guaranteeing an intact transmission of the divine message independent of the cultural consciousness of persons.

Hodge's inductivism is finally mitigated by several factors: his refusal actually to consider any alleged "error" in the Bible, his neglect of the Calvinist insistence on the radical effects of sin upon the mind, his inability actually to distinguish inspiration from illumination on the one hand or from regeneration on the other, and his innocence concerning the relation of words, thoughts, and objects. For Hodge, it was enough to confess the Bible as God's Word, meaning that the modern reader of the Bible could be assured of encountering the very words, thoughts, and intentions of God Himself.

Benjamin Breckenridge Warfield

The significance of the role played by Benjamin Breckenridge Warfield (1851–1921) in the development of inspiration theory among evangelicals cannot be overestimated: "There is little doubt but that Warfield did more to shape recent Evangelical thinking on inspiration than any other theologian."[44] Ernest Sandeen calls him "possibly the most intellectually gifted professor ever to teach on the [Princeton Theological Seminary] faculty."[45] In contrast to Charles Hodge, who spent nearly twenty years serving in the mission field and in three American parish ministries,[46] Warfield's entire professional career was spent as a seminary professor.[47] The subject of his first published article ("Inspiration and Criticism"[48]) was also that of his last ("Inspiration"[49]). In between was "an amazing series of writings focusing on the doctrine of inspiration produced . . . with special concentration in the years 1888–1894."[50] My analysis of Warfield will focus on the doctrine which, he says, is not

> the most fundamental of Christian doctrines, nor even the first thing we prove about the Scriptures. It is the last and crowning fact as to the Scriptures. These we first prove authentic, historically credible, generally trustworthy, before we prove them inspired.[51]

Like Hodge, Warfield wants to claim that his apologetic is inductive and scientific: "We follow the inductive method. When we approach the Scriptures to ascertain their doctrine of inspiration, we proceed by collecting the whole body of relevant facts."[52] "The facts," as obviously for Warfield as for Hodge, are contained in the Bible. His inductive method is thus restricted to considering the data of Scripture, but as read by those who *presuppose* the conceptual uniformity of all that Scripture teaches: "We are certainly averse to supposing that this induction, if it reaches results not absolutely consentaneous with the teachings of Scripture itself, has done anything other than discredit those teachings, or that in discrediting them, it has escaped discrediting the doctrinal authority of Scripture."[53] That is, whatever disagrees with Scripture results from invalid assumptions about it, in particular the assumption that the uniformity of Scripture is the ground of its authority.

Upon what, then, does Warfield's doctrine of inspiration rest? It rests upon the traditional doctrine of theological anthropology accepted by nearly all Calvinist Reformers. Human beings, as creatures of God, are finite in their understandings and capacities. Even apart from the consideration of sin, therefore, humans need the revelation of God if they are properly to be able to understand anything at all, natural or supernatural.[54] The entrance of sin into the picture presents "an ethical complication"; persons need a divine self-revelation but also set themselves in opposition to it, making themselves their own gods. Revelation, therefore, is the "correlate of understanding, . . . not for its own sake, but for the sake of salvation."[55] Revelation is doubly necessary, first so that finite humans may properly know the relationship of natural things to God, their creator, and second to overcome the willful rejection of that knowledge. Revelation is thus presupposed in the doctrine of inspiration, not as a synonym for or accompaniment of divine redemption but *as* a redemptive act of God.

It will not be difficult to determine the shape of Warfield's doctrine of inspiration, then, from this understanding of the epistemic and salvific necessity of divine revelation.[56] Warfield never substantially altered the definition offered in his first published article:

> Inspiration is that extraordinary, supernatural influence (or, passively, the result of it,) exerted by the Holy Ghost on the writers of our Sacred Books, by which their words were rendered also the words of God, and, therefore, perfectly infallible.[57]

Warfield further notes that divine inspiration is supernatural (i.e., unlike poetic and artistic instances of inspiration), different from the "ordinary" activity of the Spirit in conversion and sanctification, and plenary in the sense that no biblical word is more or less important than another. He also qualifies his definition, however, remarking that it is not intended to clarify the mode of inspiration (which is "inscrutable") but only its effects: it distinguishes inspiration from revelation, it specifically rejects any "mechanical" theory, and, finally, far from being mysterious, it is on the contrary one of "the plainest facts of spiritual experience."

> This, then, is what we understand by the church doctrine:—a doctrine which claims that by a special, supernatural, extraordinary influence of the Holy Ghost, the sacred writers have been guided in their writing in such a way, as while their humanity was not superseded, it was yet so dominated that their words became

at the same time the words of God, and thus, in every case and all alike, absolutely infallible.[58]

Attention must be given to what Warfield means by the domination of the biblical author by God in the process of inspiration. Warfield's usual words used in describing this phenomenon are "superintendence" and "concursus." He describes superintendence here, as noted earlier, primarily in terms of its effects rather than its means:

> [This] conception of co-authorship implies that the Spirit's superintendence extends to the choice of words by the human authors (verbal inspiration), and preserves its product from everything inconsistent with a divine author-ship—thus securing, among other things, that entire truthfulness which is everywhere presupposed in and asserted for Scripture by the Biblical writ-ers (inerrancy) . . . . [This] has always been the core of the Church doctrine of inspiration.[59]

Inspiration, then, is seen as a cooperative effort, but not between equals. Rather, it is a cooperative effort that must account for four elements which Warfield takes as irrefutable: God's primary authorship, human sinfulness and fallibility, the demonstrable inerrancy of the "texts," and the authority which those texts exercise in the church.

Although he concentrates on the effects of inspiration, Warfield does not completely ignore the means. His account of inspiration is logically located between seeing it as analogous to sanctification and as analogous to mechanical dictation, both of which he denies as being isomorphic with inspiration. Inspiration differs from the "ordinary" operation of the Spirit in sanctification in that it is an immediate divine activity.[60] It is incompatible with mechanistic theories of dictation because such theories fail to account adequately for the distinctly personal or human characteristics of the "organs of revelation."[61] In this middle ground falls Warfield's discussion of the "concursive" mode of divine inspiration. We shall inspect this middle ground from two perspectives: exegetical and systematic-conceptual.

Warfield begins "The Biblical Idea of Inspiration"[62] by noting the near universal misunderstanding of that text which is primarily cited in inspi-ration discussions: 2 Timothy 3:16.[63] "The Greek word in this passage— *theopneustos*—very distinctly does not mean 'inspired of God.' The Greek term has . . . nothing to say of *in*spiring or *in*spiration; it speaks only of a 'spiring' or 'spiration.'"[64] This certifies the conclusion that one of the most explicit biblical statements concerning inspiration allows only that the Scriptures are the product of God; nothing is said about the mode of divine production. For greater specificity regarding the means of that peculiar activ-ity, Warfield turns to 2 Peter 1:19–21.[65] Here he explores the meaning of *phero* in order to underscore the nature of human instrumentality in the production of Scripture. The following passage is puzzling, though, if the reader remembers Warfield's rejection of dictation theories:

> The term used here [*pheromenoi*] is a very specific one. It is not to be confounded with guiding, or directing, or controlling, or even leading in the full sense of that word. It goes beyond all such terms, in assigning the effect produced specifically to the active agent. What is "borne" is taken up by the "bearer," and conveyed by the "bearer's" power, not its own, to the "bearer's" goal, not its own. The men who spoke from God are here declared, therefore, to have been taken up by the Holy Spirit and brought by His power to the goal of His choosing. The things which they spoke under this operation of the Spirit were therefore His things, not theirs.[66]

This article, written toward the end of Warfield's life (1915), denied all human contributions to the actual content of Scripture except for those of style and personality.[67] "There is, therefore, . . . not, indeed, a human element or ingredient in Scripture, and much less human divisions or sections of Scripture, but a human side or aspect to Scripture. . . . Scripture is the product of man, but only of man speaking from God and under such a control of the Holy Spirit as that in their speaking they are 'borne' by Him."[68] Warfield's *concursus* is in fact very one-sided. At no place in his exegetical analysis is any consideration given to a genuine, unambiguously *human* contribution or initiative. It is to be wondered why a bifocal concept like concursus was chosen in the first place.

The reader's puzzlement does not abate when Warfield turns to a more systematic treatment of "concursive inspiration."[69] His most deliberate analysis of the various articles within *The Inspiration and Authority of the Bible* attempts to account for what may be called the psychology of the inspired writers. Warfield first recounts how God prepares those whom He will move to write in ways that are "physical, intellectual, [and] spiritual," a preparation which "must have had its beginning in their remote ancestors." This is the "providential preparation" that is the standard Reformed manner of treating the manifestation of God's sovereignty in the ordinary operation of the world; it is through means and is therefore nonmiraculous and in fact nonextraordinary.[70] But clearly providence alone cannot account for the extraordinary quality of the Scriptures, encountered in but not limited to the authority which they exercise in the church. What does explain their unique characteristics is the *additamentum* that is technically called "inspiration." This is an immediate action of God upon the biblical writer "which takes effect at the very point of the writing of Scripture . . . with the effect of giving to the resultant Scripture a specifically supernatural character."[71] This is, in effect, what the reader wanted: a clear statement of the miraculous origin of the Bible, purged of all human elements, which are simply overridden by the divine operation. Unfortunately, in his next sentence, Warfield takes back what he has just given: "the mode of operation of this Divine activity . . . is . . . in full accord with the analogy of the Divine operations in other spheres of its activities, in providence and grace alike."[72] With this his conceptual work is finished.

Warfield presents an equivocal doctrine of inspiration. His account cannot determine whether inspiration is finally a mediate or immediate activity, yet he believes that a decision must be made between these alternatives. He is unwilling to accept a doctrine of Scripture in which genuine human participation is allowed, both because such a doctrine could not explain the divine effects that the Bible exercises upon and within the church and because the (salvific) necessity of the Bible does not allow the patient to provide the remedy. But Warfield equally cannot accept a doctrine of Scripture which requires the immediate activity of God, because such a doctrine entails some form of mechanical dictation theory and the consequent utter passivity of the human instrument.[73] Warfield's uneasiness is obvious in the structure of his presentation here and elsewhere,[74] where the reader notices that he moves *from* the context of the immediate *to* the context of the mediate and never the reverse. Warfield is caught between what were for him two empirical poles: the inerrancy and authority of the Bible on the one hand and the results of anthropological and psychological observations on the other. Like Hodge, he was unable finally to decide between them because he never considered the possibility of divine activity working through nondivine, and therefore fallible, means. That is, he did not consider the Bible itself as a sacrament, a genuine creaturely product which is at the same time genuinely able to convey the divine initiative.

There are probably few names so closely associated with the concept and the apologetic significance of the "autographs" as that of Warfield. Whether this is because he generated their apologetic usefulness[75] or simply because he made explicit what had long been implicit in the discussion concerning biblical authority,[76] what is of interest to us is that "Most of the arguments advanced by . . . Evangelicals owe an enormous debt to his way of approaching the subject."[77] Thus, it is instructive to examine the apologetic use that Warfield made of the autographs since, justifiably or not, his is the name most closely associated with the popularity of this theological construct.

As we have seen, Charles Hodge estimated the significance of errors in the Bible as "flecks of sandstone in the marble of the Parthenon."[78] Warfield refused to make even this small concession. "A proved error in Scripture contradicts not only our doctrine, but the Scripture claims, and therefore its inspiration in making those claims."[79] Bearing in mind his theological location of inspiration as the "last and crowning fact" of the doctrine of

Scripture, this sentence would appear to mean that the *demonstration* of an error[80] would count against that immediate activity of the Holy Spirit by which all biblical assertions could be read as direct divine assertions. Or, to say the same thing in a different way, since scriptural authority and error were logically incompatible for Warfield, a demonstrable error in the Bible would count against the authority of the Bible. Since, however, the Bible is in fact authoritative in church practice, it must also be in fact inerrant, and if in fact inerrant, then in principle inerrant. Any error anywhere would invalidate this reasoning, because those passages that directly relate to inspiration (2 Timothy 3:16, 2 Peter 1:19–21, and John 10:34[81]) were read as applying to the whole of the canon and not just to restricted parts of it.[82]

Clearly, however, the inerrancy of the biblical texts could not be argued with respect to contemporary copies of the Scriptures. It is not that Warfield admits to "errors" in these copies.[83] Instead, the divine protection of inspiration extends only to the actual words placed on the page by the inspired writer, and not to translations or copies. In this way, Warfield restricts the scope of the "process" of inspiration to the literal moment of scripting and thus to the autographs. He has already denied any antecedent significance to inspiration by carefully distinguishing between providence and inspiration. With this move, he also denies any subsequent immediate interventions to safeguard the divine characteristics of the texts. What remains is an immediate, temporal intervention in the life of a human being the effect of which is to guarantee that that person's written product will reflect only such human attributes as have no specific religious significance. Abraham's comment about the use and the effects of dictation seems justified.[84]

Like Hodge before him, Warfield thus appears to follow an inductive model in his approach to biblical inspiration. In "The Church Doctrine of Inspiration" (1894), for example, he recalls what is presumably his own story of coming to trust the Bible. In a passage as moving as it is methodologically significant, he writes:

> We are all of us members in particular of the body of Christ which we call the church: and the life of the church, and the faith of the church, and the thought of the church are our natural heritage. We know that, as Christian men, we approach this Holy Book—how unquestioningly we receive its statements of fact, bow before its enunciations of duty, tremble before its threatenings, and rest upon its promises. . . . [Our] memory will easily recall those happier days when we stood a child at our Christian mother's knee, with lisping lips following the words which her slow finger traced upon this open page, —words which were her support in every trial and, as she fondly trusted, were to be our guide throughout life. Mother church was speaking to us in that voice, commending to us her vital faith in the Word of God. . . . In such scenes as these is revealed the vital faith of the people of God in the surety and trustworthiness of the word of God.[85]

As both Sandeen and Parsons note, however, "Warfield never actually *uses* such an argument to provide authentication for a [biblical] statement."[86]

In the end, then, Warfield's deductivism was even more pronounced than that of his mentor. His first detailed doctrine concerning the legitimate parameters of inspiration theory never changed:

> With these presumptions and in this spirit let it (1) be proved that each alleged discrepant statement certainly occurred in the original autograph of the sacred book in which it is said to be found. (2) Let it be proved that the interpretation which occasions the apparent discrepancy is the one which the passage was evidently intended to bear. It is not sufficient to show a difficulty, which may spring out of our defective knowledge of the circumstances. The true meaning must be definitely and certainly ascertained, and then shown to be irreconcilable with other known truth. (3) Let it be proved that the true sense of some part of the original autograph is directly and necessarily inconsistent with some certainly-known fact of history or truth of science, or some other statement of Scripture certainly ascertained and interpreted. We believe that it can be shown that this has never yet been successfully done in the case of one single alleged instance of error in the WORD OF GOD.[87]

The theological and exegetical restrictions placed upon the inductive task completely guaranteed that no error could ever be charged against the Bible. Only the third condition mentioned here is capable of being implemented even in principle. The likelihood of its being used in fact is diminished by its logical dependence upon the prior two conditions whose practical demonstrability is nil in both cases.

Warfield's approach explains the normativity of Scripture by means of a theory which, paradoxically, ends up denying the *actual* normativity of Scripture. Both Hodge and Warfield testify to the "volumes" of discrepancies and errors alleged against the Bible, but neither confronts any serious discrepancy at the exegetical level.[88] Thus, exegesis is completely dominated by systematic considerations. In a startlingly clear affirmation of this domination, Warfield asks, "The issue is not, what does the Bible teach? but, Is what the Bible teaches true?"[89] A year earlier, writing more expansively upon the same subject, he contrasted "two ways of approaching the study of the inspiration of the Bible." The first operates by comparing the "facts [of] the Bible as ascertained by Biblical criticism and exegesis" against "the doctrine of inspiration taught by the Bible as applicable to itself." Warfield's explanation of the second way will be cited at length:

> The other method proceeds by seeking the doctrine of inspiration in the first instance through a comprehensive induction from the facts as to the structure and contents of the Bible, as ascertained by critical and exegetical processes, treating all these facts as co-factors of the same rank for the induction. If in this process

the facts of structure and the facts embedded in the record of Scripture . . . alone are considered, it would be difficult to arrive at a precise doctrine of inspiration, at the best: though, as we have already pointed out, a degree and kind of accuracy might be vindicated for the Scriptures which might lead us to suspect and to formulate as the best account of it, some divine assistance to the writers' memory, mental processes and expression. If the Biblical facts and teaching are taken as co-factors in the induction, the procedure . . . is liable to the danger of modifying the teaching by the facts without clear recognition of what is being done; the result of which would be the loss from observation of one main fact of errancy, viz., the inaccuracy of the teaching of the Scriptures as to their own inspiration. This would vitiate the whole result. . . .[90]

It will be noted that this is the approach which more closely approximates the inductive method.

In rejecting inductivism as the preferred approach because of its tendency to equate "facts with teaching" and thus risk allowing the facts to overwhelm[91] the teaching, Warfield commits a grave mistake. In principle he allows one divinely instantiated miracle ("a biblical teaching") to take precedence over other divinely instantiated miracles ("biblical facts"). By so doing, he sets one part of God's Word over other parts, which itself is a contradiction of the doctrine of plenary inspiration. But more importantly, judgment concerning the greater and lesser significance of various parts of the Bible is itself an entirely human and therefore extrabiblical operation. Surely the Bible nowhere authorizes its own compartmentalization into areas of wider and narrower significance. If such a compartmentalization has in fact occurred, then noninspired fallible humans must be responsible. If this is the result, then the entire apologetic mechanism of difficulties, inerrancy, and autographa freezes, for this mechanism has no purpose other than to insulate the original purity of the Scriptures against the encroachments of self-serving humans. Warfield's use of Scripture subordinates exegesis to prior, and therefore "external," considerations. But this is precisely the charge he had leveled against his opponents. It is not entirely unexpected, then, to observe increasing resistance among evangelicals to the use of this mechanism as they grew more familiar with its implications.[92]

John Warwick Montgomery

John Warwick Montgomery (born 1931) has earned degrees in library research, philosophy and philosophical historiography, church history, theology, and law, and he is an ordained Lutheran pastor. His written contributions to each of these disciplines are voluminous. It is, however, as an apologist for the Christian faith that he is of interest here. I shall demonstrate here that the constant theme occurring throughout all of his apologetic work is intellectual "certainty." More particularly, it is a religious certainty analogous to that generated by history and philosophy. Montgomery's contention is that biblical inspiration and inerrancy are the only possible warrants which can account for the certainty to which Christian believers are called and which they in fact possess.

Like the other theologians discussed in this chapter, Montgomery claims to reason inductively in theological as well as extratheological areas.[93] Thus, the first task of this section is to explain the methodological approach which Montgomery says that he follows in all of his various areas of specialty. Fortunately for the reader, he has provided a succinct account of his method of inquiry. Second, this section will address itself in particular to his "inductive inerrancy"[94] in order to determine whether he is faithful to his own inductive method. That is, I shall ask whether his own theory of inspiration can be counted as successful when measured against the standards he gives to his reader. I shall conclude that it cannot.

Montgomery defends the belief that the Bible is sufficient to account for religious certainty because it is historically accurate in all details. Therefore, all of its claims concerning Jesus are true as a matter of history, independent of the consideration of personal faith. For him, Christian belief is identical with clear thinking about the past. He fails to notice, however, that clear thinking in theology, as in science and history, is grounded in judgments of the mind, and judgments are by definition located outside of the Bible. Thus, regardless of the question of the Bible's historical accuracy, religious certainty is grounded in a judgment about the Bible, and not in the Bible itself.

In "The Theologian's Craft: A Discussion of Theory Formation and Theory Testing in Theology,"[95] Montgomery presents an explicitly normative statement concerning the relationship between science and theology and the implications of this relationship for those intending to do appropriate theological activity. He begins by noting that the uncertainty most people feel with respect to what theologians do is not caused by a lack of perceptiveness but the opposite: they are *correctly* suspicious of the irreducible diversity of the things that theologians do. Montgomery turns to "the field of science" in order to "examine the essential nature of theories [in] the discipline in which they have been most thoroughly discussed"[96] so as better to explain what theologians do. Implicit in this strategy is the assumption that "science and theology form and test their respective theories in the same way,"[97] an assumption he examines only after explicit scientific theorizing has been analyzed.

Montgomery begins by noting that contemporary philosophy of science largely accepts Wittgenstein's "net" analogy.[98] A net is a conceptual construct which attempts to represent or reflect reality in such a manner as to make that reality understandable to the mind. The net itself is made up of observations, hypotheses, and theories, each of which is able to account for segments of external reality with lesser or greater degrees of success. The ultimate criterion of success is "fit," that is, whether the proposed ("hypothetical") explanation accounts for the widest relevant range of external reality. Fit is tested by predictability, the ability to reconstitute reality artificially or experimentally so that it mirrors the original given reality.

Montgomery draws two conclusions from this analogy. The first is that "theories do not create facts; rather, they attempt to relate existent facts properly."[99] This appears merely to restate simple inductivism, but Montgomery goes on to the second conclusion which is that neither strict induction nor strict deduction can account for the nature and success of scientific discoveries since the Enlightenment and especially in the twentieth century. "Instead of seeking monolithic explanation of scientific method, let us, with Max Black, 'think of science as a concrescence, a growing together of variable, interacting, mutually reinforcing factors contributing to a development organic in character.'"[100] Science has operated most successfully when scientists have tested deductions by inductions and inductions by deductions, with the criterion of success always remaining compatibility with actuality and the advance of human understanding of the real world.[101]

"Imagination" plays a crucial role in science; it can be seen as the "connecting link" between induction and deduction.[102] At times, the "beauty" or "fit" of the conceptual theory with respect to objects in reality is so great as actually to constitute evidence of its own applicability. At other times, theory is predictive in the sense of far outstripping present means of experimental verification. The relevant point is that the mind contributes a distinct datum to scientific inquiry, a "conceptual Gestalt"[103] apart from which scientific progress would be severely restricted and perhaps unthinkable.

Montgomery now considers whether the analogy between science and theology is legitimate: "Is not theology a unique realm of the 'spirit,' unscientific by its very nature? . . . What has . . . the Laboratory [to do] with the Church?"[104] His response is the same as the one given by Hodge. The "objective" data which form the basis for theological theorizing are contained in the Bible, and thus the task of the theologian is "to provide conceptual Gestalts (doctrines, dogmas) which will 'fit the facts' and properly reflect the norms of Holy Scripture."[105] Theologians, in other words, largely do what scientists do. Using the discipline of history as his scientific paradigm, he claims that

> Christianity is unique in claiming intrinsic, not merely extrinsic, connection with the empirical reality which is the subject of scientific investigation. Christianity is a *historical* religion—historical in the very special sense that its entire revela-

tional content is wedded to historical manifestations of Divine power. The pivot
of Christian theology is the biblical affirmation that *ho Logos sarx egeneto* (John
1:14).[106]

Theology, like history, is a science. Although it is more than just a science,
it will at the very least utilize those concepts common to the natural sciences
which have proven to be the most successful in understanding the real world.

As a science, theology must employ a means of verification in order to
be successful. As we have seen, the criterion for success in the natural
sciences is fit with respect to observable reality, that is, how well a theory explains the facts needing explanation.[107] Theology employs the same
criterion. Borrowing Ian Ramsey's analogy of the shoe and the foot (corre-
sponding to Wittgenstein's net and objective reality), Montgomery quotes
Ramsey's description of a "successful" shoe: "The test of a shoe is measured
by its ability to match a wide range of phenomena, by its overall success in
meeting a variety of needs. Here is what I might call the method of empirical
fit which is displayed by theological theorizing."[108] We might say that theory
(doctrine and dogma) in religion is successful when it explains biblical data
in ways understandable to those desiring to understand them.

Clearly, it is essential to understand exactly what in theology corresponds to the "foot," the objective reality or data in the scientific realm.
Montgomery's response here is that "revelational experience" stands as the
object of theological inquiry. He recognizes, however, that this phrase is
ambiguous. It might refer to any of at least four alternatives: "Reason, the
Church, Christian Experience, and Scriptural Revelation" or the Bible.[109]
The first three are excluded both individually and collectively. Reason[110] is
rejected because it is either tautologous and therefore noninformative concerning the real world[111] or because reason alone cannot discriminate between
true and false religions. Reason can "yield atheistic ideologies almost as easily as deistic theologies."[112] The church is rejected as "court of last resort
for determining what are or what are not genuine data for theologizing,"
because an infinite regress is implied: how can one be certain that the interpretation rendered by an infallible church does not itself require an infallible
interpretation, and so on? In addition, there is no biblical mandate for such
authority. And Christian experience must be rejected as the "objective datum"
of theologizing precisely because it is not objective. Christian experience is
nothing but the collective experience of various subjective individuals. But
the judgment that the experience of these individuals should be deemed normative is independent of and logically prior to that experience. If it is not
independent but is somehow located *in* the experience, then the "naturalist fallacy" of confusing description and normativity, "isness" and "oughtness," is committed.[113] "Paul Tillich argues with irrefutable cogency that

'insight into the human situation destroys every theology which makes experience an independent source instead of a dependent medium of systematic theology.'"[114]

All three candidates are rejected for the same reason: "all multiple-source views of the subject matter of theology are . . . unstable."[115] Ultimately, if not sooner, conflict arises between the dual sources, for example, between the church and the Bible in Roman Catholicism or between experience and the Bible in liberal Protestantism. Where such conflict arises, however, the criterion or standard chosen to resolve it itself becomes the final source. "Multiple source approaches to the subject matter of theology thus logically—whether one likes it or not—reduce to single source interpretations."[116] "Thus we arrive at the Bible—the source by which Reason, Church and Religious Experience can and must be evaluated theologically. We reach this point not simply by process of elimination, but more especially because only Scripture can be validated as a genuine source of theological truth."[117]

The claim here is that Scripture is *norma normans non normata;* the Bible alone is ultimately normative in matters of reason, practice, and experience. We shall now examine Montgomery's claims concerning Scripture by reflecting upon the analogy between scientific and theological activity.

The first point to notice is that there is no relevant analogy at all between the givenness of natural data in science and the givenness of Scriptural data in theology. Wittgenstein's net analogy emphasizes that it is *not* obvious how to understand and conceive of the natural world and that various alternatives (hypotheses and ultimately theories) suggest competing ways of conceptualizing it until such time as the criteria of fit, predictability, and experimentation are able to judge among better and worse theories. The data of the natural world are therefore "objective" only in the sense that they constitute the foundation to which observation statements, hypotheses, and theories must be faithful,[118] and not in the sense that they are easily and objectively understood. The infrastructure of observation statements, hypotheses, and theories is constructed with the aid of the imagination, not in order to create the world of facts but to create the world of understandable or conceivable facts. The net analogy does not presume that there are no facts until nets create them. Rather, it reflects the scientific community's (temporary) uncertainty over how best to conceive of the structure and relations of those facts.

Such, however, is not at all the status of biblical facts in Montgomery's scheme. As we have just seen, Montgomery believes that the Bible is the "single source" from which theologians obtain their data. But in spite of his insistence that "What Nature is to the scientific theorizer, the Bible is to the theologian,"[119] biblical facts are significantly different from their natural counterparts. For one thing, Montgomery sees the Bible as "self-interpreting"; it provides not only facts and data but also the "norms" by which to understand and interpret them.[120] In other words, the Bible, rightly read, provides the theories by which all religious data are to be understood. But where is the relevant analogy in science? The storehouse of objective data in the natural realm does not include hypotheses and theories; these are the contributions of human imagination, which work to organize those data into conceivable groupings so that the mind can comprehend them. In theology, however, we have seen that Montgomery explicitly rejects the contribution of human imagination as being a "second source" in competition with the source of scriptural revelation. The science of theology is thus seen to be entirely reproductive or repetitive. Theologians simply recapitulate the given data by means of norms and principles which are not only elements within the given but are understood as such by the mind of the theologian. Perhaps this is actually what Montgomery intends to say, but if so, why bother with the lengthy and irrelevant analogy from science?

A second puzzling question occurs to the reader while reflecting on Montgomery's use of the naturalistic fallacy. To recall the point: Montgomery had charged those who wished to see religious experience as a legitimate source of theological data with committing that logical fallacy because they confused description with prescription, "isness" with "oughtness." "How is one to know that the divine and not the demonic is operating in the given experience?"[121] He responds with the point noted earlier, that some independent or objective check is needed, "a source of theological data outside of [religious experience], by which to judge it."[122] He finds this check in the Bible. But how does he know that he has found it there? Most theologians answer this question by referring in various ways to the "faith" of the Christian person, but Montgomery does not. Instead, he turns to the discussion of the objective, historical credibility of the Bible as that which ultimately validates the certainty of Christian knowledge.

In his book *The Shape of the Past: An Introduction to Philosophical Historiography,*[123] Montgomery lists those elements of the "empirical method as applied to history [by which] one can inductively validate the Christian revelation claim and the biblical view of total history":[124]

1. On the basis of accepted principles of textual and historical analysis, the Gospel records are found to be trustworthy historical documents—a primary source evidence for the life of Christ.

2. In these records, Jesus exercises divine prerogatives and claims to be God in human flesh; and He rests His claims on His forthcoming resurrection.

3. In all four Gospels, Christ's bodily resurrection is described in minute detail; Christ's resurrection evidences His deity.

4. The fact of the resurrection cannot be discounted on *a priori,* philosophical grounds; miracles are impossible only if one so defines them—but such definition rules out proper historical investigation.

5. If Christ is God, then He speaks the truth concerning the absolute divine authority of the Old Testament and of the soon-to-be-written New Testament; concerning His death for the sins of the world; and concerning the nature of man and of history.

6. It follows from the preceding that all Biblical assertions bearing on philosophy of history are to be regarded as revealed truth, and that all human attempts at historical interpretation are to be judged for truth-value on the basis of harmony with Scriptural revelation.

The point of interest here for our purposes is not so much whether Montgomery is historically justified in making statements such as 1 above, whether statement 2 is merely a variant of John Hick's discredited "eschatological verification" scheme,[125] whether any dispassionate reading of Paul and the Gospels could lead to statement 3,[126] or whether the conditional clause in statement 5 is as straightforward and logical as Montgomery asserts.[127] I believe that there are serious theological difficulties with each of these statements (except for 4, which is purely methodological and therefore not a theological or historical assertion). Rather, it is that the "shape" of his argument is exactly the opposite of the kind of argumentation employed by philosophers of science, arguments which Montgomery used to illuminate the meaning and validity of theological science. Wittgenstein and Ramsey both took data or facts to be objective not in the sense of being knowable (much less known) with certainty by the mind a priori, but rather as being that to which the mind constantly must return in its attempt to organize what it encounters outside itself into knowable units of information understandable to itself. Imagination, the source of that which is "new" to the observations made by the mind, is thus indispensable to the organization of observations into knowledge. Montgomery's method reverses this process and in so doing negates the contribution of imagination altogether. Instead of the mind contributing to observations in such a manner as (ultimately) to arrive at certainty, the mind begins with the certainty of biblical data, accepts the norms or principles within those data as authoritative and justified indicators of how to evaluate them, and then simply draws inferences and conclusions from them.[128] The contribution of the mind, therefore, is analogous to the person who encounters true major and minor premises in a syllogism and "contributes" a justified conclusion. Whatever that contribution is, it is hardly imagination.

The reader would thus need to know whence arises Montgomery's "certainty" concerning the objective givenness of the biblical data. We have already seen that it cannot arise from a person's own experience since, for Montgomery, this would constitute an illicit subjectivism.[129] But it also cannot arise from outside the person, even though that is where he would have us believe it arises. Unintentionally, presumably, he has already told us why the warrant for theological certainty cannot reside outside the person. In previously rejecting the "collective" appropriateness of reason, the church, or experience as legitimate loci of theological data, he said that they are illegitimate because the judgment of the mind required to adjudicate between tensions generated by any pairs of these multiple sources would itself become the final source of acceptable religious data. So too here. The judgment of the mind which accepts the legitimacy of the Bible as the only valid source of religious data and norms logically antedates the Bible as that source and thus is shown as the source of whatever certainty the person experiences with the Bible. "Certainty" is a category of the mind, not of external reality. When the mind accepts a particular book as being of ultimate religious certainty and authority, it is the mind that judges it to be certain and not the book which somehow presses certainty onto the mind from without.

Montgomery's elaborate and elegantly argued case for the similarity of the natural and theological enterprises collapses not so much because he fails to understand either science or theology,[130] but rather because, once having presented the character of natural science in a manner which reflects the conclusions of credible philosophers of science,[131] he fails to apply it to theology. He claims that a genuine analogy exists, but he shows the precise opposite.

We turn now to an examination of Montgomery's explanation and defense of the doctrine of "inductive inerrancy."[132] He begins with James Orr's contention that each great epoch of church history has had to "come to grips with one particular doctrine of crucial significance both for that day and for the subsequent history of the Church."[133] Montgomery believes that "the doctrinal problem which, above all others, demands resolution in the modern Church is that of the authority of Holy Scriptures. All other issues of belief today pale before this issue."[134] In particular, the issue at the root of the authority question is whether inspiration and inerrancy can be split. Montgomery judges that most current theologians agree that they should be, whereas he believes that they cannot. It is not just the case that they ought not be separated, but rather that they logically cannot be separated. He finds the warrant for this logical "cannot" in "certain new techniques derived from the realm of analytical philosophy."[135]

Montgomery finds two distinct contextual causes for the current skepticism over the inerrancy of the Bible. The first is metaphysical dualism, "the venerable philosophical position . . . which in one form or other has always claimed that the Absolute cannot be fully manifested in the phenomenal world."[136] Representative dualists he cites are Plato, Reformation Calvinists, Kant, and Hegel. The second and more serious cause of skepticism, though, is existentialism, which is "the redefinition of truth in *personal,* as opposed to propositional, terms."[137] Existentialism attempts to overcome the "subject-object distinction" by pointing out that "'existence,' as manifested in personal relationships, precedes and surpasses in quality, 'essence,' i.e., formal propositional assertions or descriptions concerning reality."[138] Both positions tend to weaken the significance of the inerrancy position. Dualism rejects the idea that God could be present anywhere in the natural world, and existentialism rejects the idea that God could be present by means of linguistic propositions.

Montgomery turns to classical verificationism as his conceptual resource for criticizing dualism and existentialism. Verificationism is the attempt to demonstrate the meaningfulness of propositions by affirming that the only statements which can be called meaningful are those whose assertions concerning the world can be tested as being either true or false. He quotes A. J. Ayer, one of the earliest proponents of verificationism:

> The criterion which we use to test the genuineness of apparent statements of fact is the criterion of verifiability. We say that a sentence is factually significant to any given person, if, and only if, he knows how to verify the proposition which it purports to express—that is, if he knows what observations would lead him, under certain conditions, to accept that proposition as being true, or reject it as being false.[139]

Whatever cannot be verified according to this criterion is declared meaningless or nonsense. Montgomery applies the verifiability criterion first to dualism and existentialism and then to the claim of modern theologians that biblical inspiration is meaningful when considered apart from inerrancy.

Montgomery distills the variously stated anti-inerrancy statements into two representative classes. The first is that "Holy Scripture is inspired, not in conveying inerrant propositions about God and the world, but in acting as a vehicle for true Christian existential experience."[140] Within this is represented the existentialist hermeneutic of Rudolf Bultmann, who understands the referent of biblical assertions to be not God, but the human subject's experience of God.[141] Montgomery rejects this alternative, first, because of its own inconsistency; it purports to do away with propositional revelation by means of propositions. Second, he rejects it because of the naturalist fallacy: how can one be certain that his or her experience is *Christian* experience if propositional and doctrinal articulations of Christian truth are ruled out of court?

The second type of wedge driven between inspiration and inerrancy is one which attempts somehow to specify the purpose of Scripture so that the various kinds of errors alleged to be in it could not count against this purpose. Montgomery responds by asking how the (religious) purpose of Scripture is to be abstracted from the historical, scientific, sociological, and moral elements of Scripture without making the distinguishing criterion itself the "real" Scripture. And if *(per impossible)* this distinction could be made, how could these "real" statements be shown to be inspired in such a way that did not also apply, at least in principle, to what was pruned away? This position is meaningless, he believes, because it follows from a dualistic presumption which denies any penetration of the divine into the human, and therefore also ends up denying inspiration even of the theological or religious statements of the Bible. Montgomery's major warrant for both objections, then, is that there is both a soteriological *and* an epistemological significance to the Christian notion of Incarnation.[142] That is, the incarnation shows that human thinking processes per se, as well as the human soul in general, are set against God and are thus in need of divine forgiveness and conversion.

There are difficulties in Montgomery's account of inductive inerrancy which obstruct its success in accounting for the certainty which he claims attends a proper reading of the text. Two objections are in order. The first involves his puzzling dependence upon the verificationist scheme of Ayer, who had claimed that the meaningfulness of a given sentence was relative to one's ability to verify it, or at least to know the conditions for verifying it. This means that the meaning of a sentence is strictly dependent upon its ability to be tested.[143] Many have noted that the verifiability principle itself is not able to be tested and thus is meaningless according to itself.[144] This objection is relevant in particular to the "validating elements" of Christian theology noted earlier, where Montgomery's case seems to boil down to Jesus having spoken the truth because he was God, with the latter claim being a true claim as validated by the supreme miracle of rising from the dead. But if Ayer's verification procedure is accepted here, then simple eyewitness reports are not sufficient for a genuine validation of this event as Montgomery supposes in his statement 3, since then their reports would require validation, and so on. What would be sufficient would be empirical repetition, which in the nature of the case cannot be expected.

The second objection to Montgomery's apologetic is that it too sets up an extrabiblical criterion as final test of the meaningfulness of religious statements which, according to Montgomery himself, logically becomes "scripture" to those who hold it. The verifiability principle is "external" not just to those who use it but also to the Bible itself. Montgomery claims that the biblical writers presupposed it and that modern readers may do so as well. But this reply substantially changes the argument. No longer is it the text of Scripture which is normative for Christian theology, but rather the presuppositions of its authors. Inspiration thus has to do not with the text, which is publicly available today, but with interior mental processes which, if they were ever available, certainly are not today. According to his argument, inductive inerrancy is a characteristic of the text which is apparent to all clear thinkers who are not predisposed to reject it. According to his explanation of the argument, however, inductive inerrancy is a characteristic of the marriage of the verifiability principle and the presuppositions of the biblical authors, neither of which is a textual element. It is therefore fair to conclude that Montgomery's account of religious certainty fails to show how that certainty is based in the Bible.

Montgomery sets himself an energetic task: to account for the certainty of Christian faith based upon the truthfulness of the Bible as determined both by generally accepted historical principles and by the verificationist discoveries of twentieth-century philosophy of science. Even if he had been successful, however, and there is good reason to think that he was not, it seems to miss the point of religious certainty. All that Montgomery's apologetic intends to do is demonstrate the reliability of the biblical authors as historians since, as we have seen, he takes their writings as straightforward historical assertions whose truthfulness can be judged entirely apart from the consideration of "faith." But it is a huge leap from saying that they are reliable historians to the profession of belief in Jesus as the Christ and as God incarnate. Historical accuracy per se is not a distinctively Christian criterion, and telling the truth in matters historical is not identical with Christian faith. Faith is self-involving, and as Donald Evans reminds us, self-involving claims "involve a speaker logically in something more than a mere assent to fact."[145] Typically, that "something more" is commitment to some kind of present and future action, whereas the only commitment called for by "assent to fact" is that which affirms the correspondence between a given sentence and a given state of affairs. In claiming correctness for the biblical authors, Montgomery fails to inspect how their correct words are perceived as that kind of truth which would lead a reader in the present to commit his or her life to a certain set of actions and beliefs within a community of faith. Historical accuracy alone cannot elicit an appropriate confession of faith.

Edward John Carnell

Edward John Carnell (1919–1967) was professor of Christian apologetics at Fuller Theological Seminary in Pasadena, California, from 1948 until his death. He served as seminary president from 1954 to 1959. He enjoyed a near-paradigmatic evangelical education: the son of a Baptist pastor, he earned the B.A. in philosophy under Gordon Clark at Wheaton College, the divinity degree in apologetics under Cornelius Van Til at Westminster Seminary, the Th.D. from Harvard Divinity School ("The Concept of Dialectic in the Theology of Reinhold Niebuhr," 1948),[146] and the Ph.D. from Boston University ("The Problem of Verification in Soren Kierkegaard," 1949). He was also professor of philosophy and religion at Gordon College and Gordon Divinity School immediately before his appointment at Fuller.

Carnell is of interest here because of the deliberate way in which he attempts to utilize contemporary philosophy to articulate and defend his understanding of Christian faith. His works are intentionally systematic in nature. We have already seen similar methodological interests in Hodge, Warfield, and Montgomery. For Hodge and Warfield, the Bible is to theology what the world is to natural science: the storehouse of data needing rearrangement into readily understandable patterns. For Montgomery, the Bible is also a storehouse, but this time of historical claims which are identical with God's understanding of history, are therefore inerrantly true, and thus simply need to be read with an unprejudiced mind in order to be understood faithfully. Each of these three authors sees divine activity terminating directly in the Bible rather than in persons. Inspiration is thus a category which begins with God and ends with the scripting of the text, with the result being that the text is objectively true. Inspiration appears to be an ad hoc explanation of a miraculous act which these authors would have explained as dictation had they been allowed.

Although Carnell is a deductivist as well, he is not as strict as Warfield and Montgomery in that he allows for extrabiblical knowledge to inform one's understanding of the Bible. We saw this in Hodge, who agreed that contemporary scientific discoveries could and did contribute to the interpretation of Genesis. For Carnell, the extrabiblical criterion is logic.

In his work *An Introduction to Christian Apologetics: A Philosophic Defense of Trinitarian-Theistic Faith*,[147] Carnell claims that Christianity is warranted as true by its "systematic consistency." Systematic consistency includes both empirical and logical referents, although I shall show that his ultimate warrant is logic alone. The importance of showing this lies not so much in pointing out an inconsistency in Carnell as in noting that logic is an extrabiblical phenomenon which itself constitutes the criterion for determining the truth of biblical statements. Unlike Montgomery, who thought that he could find both data *and* norms in the Bible, Carnell is willing to find those norms elsewhere, which at least introduces the possibility of seeing inspiration outside the Bible as well.

Although statements in the *Apologetics* which deal more directly with inspiration are relatively few, they are nonetheless fascinating, especially Carnell's discussion of errors in the Bible.[148] He has a more moderate position concerning biblical errors than do Warfield or Montgomery. On the one hand, error is incompatible with God's character and anything God does. On the other hand, present copies of the Bible contain errors. Such errors, however, do not restrict God's ability to work through the Bible but instead may become the very means by which God brings about repentance.

Religion, for Carnell, is the human response to "soul-sorrow," the realization of the "insatiable desire for self-preservation [in the face of] the realities of a death-doomed body and an impersonal universe."[149] Because there is no area of life which can escape these realities, it is imperative for religion to be on the surest possible footing as it suggests responses both to account for and to overcome this fatal realization. Thus, "one can easily detect that the basic problem of religion is *verification,* since it is always theoretically possible that what has been conceived to be God . . . is in reality nothing but the fruit of an auto-projection."[150]

Three types of verification systems are considered. The first is "demonstrative" or logical proof. This approach is useful in that it helps one "to segregate the true from the false" in systems of thought. It is not sufficient or ultimate, though, because "reality cannot be connected by formal logic alone. . . . Logical truth cannot pass into material truth until the facts of life are introduced into the picture."[151] This factor necessitates a second systematic approach, "inductive" proof. This system of proof deals with the "concrete history" that comprises much of human life, such as weighing, measuring, experimenting, and the like. The risk involved in inductive proof is that it can only be probable proof; it cannot account for the certainty which the mind desires in the act of knowing. What would be optimum would be the uniting of these two, a union Carnell discovers in the third system, proof by "systematic consistency" or "coherence."

Systematic consistency applies to all experience. Formal (or logical) verifiability ensures the "universality and necessity" of this method, and material (or inductive) verifiability ensures its "relevance to the world in which we live."[152] Carnell does not, however, explain the method of systematic consistency in such a way as to give equal weight to both the formal and the material aspects. Instead, as I will show, the ultimate criterion of meaningfulness is logical consistency as tested by the law of contradiction.

Systematic consistency is presented as that method which alone is able to account for all of human experience, which Carnell defines as the "total breadth of human consciousness which embraces the entire rational, volitional and emotional life of man."[153] As its name implies, there are two aspects to this method. "Consistency" implies obedience to the law of contradiction, defined in its traditional form of "A is not non-A." It is primarily a negative test and thus is "our surest test for the absence of truth."[154] That is, the law of contradiction cannot demonstrate that rabbits exist but only that rabbits, if they exist, cannot be sheep, if sheep exist. This type of proof thus stands in need of supplementation by some method of material demonstration which verifies the existence of things in the real world.

The material or real world is accounted for in the "systematic" aspect of the method of systematic consistency: "The real is whatever is, that is, whatever may be brought into our experience."[155] It deals with the actual course of events and "embraces chairs, planets, eels, and the like."[156] It is necessary to include a material component in a truth claim since, as was noted earlier, the existence of things in the real world cannot be *established* on formal grounds alone. Carnell here affirms the Kantian observation concerning concepts and percepts respectively: "validity without real facts is . . . empty (save in mathematics and logic), and the facts of experience without the formal direction of the law of contradiction are blind."[157] Thus, systematic consistency is warranted by both negative and positive characteristics as the only method of inquiry fully able to discern the truth. Truth is defined as "a quality of that judgment or proposition which, when followed out into the total witness of facts in our experience, does not disappoint our . . . expectations. . . . Truth . . . is a judgment which corresponds to things as they actually are."[158]

A Christian, however, while being fully convinced of the universal applicability of the method of systematic consistency, will not be satisfied with the definition of truth just given since it omits any reference to God: "For the Christian, God is truth because He is the author of all facts and meaning."[159] Thus, not only must "the mind of God" be brought into consideration as a formal component of truth, but it must be seen as an antecedent component as well. God is the source of all proper facts and meaning. He is, in other words, the source of all true judgments concerning the real world, and thus He is the ultimate referent of all true judgments: "Truth, for the Christian, is defined as *correspondence with the mind of God*."[160] True human judgments recapitulate divine judgments. As God not only created all things but also knows them exhaustively, the meaning that God gives to things is the meaning discovered by the method of systematic consistency: "The test for truth is systematic consistency, for God is consistent and the world that He . . . orders gives system to this consistency."[161]

We are now able to see more precisely how Carnell's explication of coherence or systematic consistency depends ultimately upon compatibility with formal validity rather than, as he asserts, a balance of formal and material validity. Two factors illustrate this assessment. The first is that both logical and material meanings[162] are adjudicated by reference to the formal law of contradiction: "The law of contradiction is so basic to meaningful thought and, consequently, to truth, for truth is concerned only with meaning, that it cannot be demonstrated. The only proof for the law is that nothing is meaningful without the law's validity being presupposed."[163] As Carnell notes, however, this is a judgment concerning meaning, and if "meaning is a property of the mind,"[164] a fortiori judgments about meaning are as well. This is the imbalance between the relative importance of formal and material factors. Material factors constitute the necessary pool or storehouse of experiences, but the formal law of contradiction is alone sufficient to discriminate true from false judgments of experience.[165] For the Carnell of the *Apologetics,* the formal law of contradiction critically evaluates fully knowable material objects and the meanings which relate those objects to each other. It thus functions as the final criterion of truth for both religious and nonreligious beliefs.

The second factor which serves to warrant the assessment that Carnell's system depends ultimately upon compatibility with formal logic is his belief that all formal and material elements are known to the mind by way of propositions. Propositions, in effect, are mediators of external reality to the mind.[166] The truth or falsity of a given proposition with respect to material objects is determined not by means of criteria which inductively relate external objects with ideas or conceptions, as one would expect, but rather by systemic coherence: "proof by coherence [is] the sticking-togetherness of our propositions."[167] Carnell points to the ancient debate between Thales and Anaximander[168] as an example of a conflict of truth claims which was settled ultimately not by exhaustive empirical demonstration but by logical coherence: "[Anaximander's] propositions stuck together better than those of Thales."[169] In addition, however, and even more to the point, propositions constitute the basis or foundation of the early Carnell's theory of knowledge. "It is in this *framework* that the Christian offers proof for his system: it sticks together. . . . God is absolute consistency."[170] Thus, it is the coherence of a given system which ultimately warrants its truthfulness, that is, its correspondence to things as they actually are. Coherence is evaluated with respect to how well propositions stick together in the mind, which is itself a function of logical consistency.[171] It does not seem unfair, therefore, to conclude that the *Apologetics* is fundamentally inconsistent in following its own proposed methodology.

We have seen that Carnell understands all truth to be grounded in the formal or logical law of contradiction. In particular, the truth of Christianity is grounded in its success in accounting for the "facts" of the real world in a way which does not violate the formal law of contradiction. Such success is tested or evaluated by the way in which the Bible's propositions concerning the real world logically adhere to each other.

In turning more directly to a consideration of Carnell's understanding of biblical inspiration, it must be noted that, in the *Apologetics* at least, he is not as concerned to build a theory of inspiration as he is to build a theory of knowledge. My examination will thus be of those relatively few passages in which he refers to the "process" of the communication of the divine character to and through the Bible. It should be expected that *what* are found to be communicated are propositions concerning the divine intentions for human life and salvation, since propositions mediate external reality to the mind.

Carnell does not intend to be original in his understanding of inspiration. Inspiration is initially defined as a "divine afflatus" or "breathing upon."[172] It is an influence exercised by God upon the biblical writers whose effect is to preserve the inerrancy of the Bible in its "spiritual prophecies and . . . historical judgments."[173] Carnell is not concerned here to clarify whether the object of afflatus is the biblical author in the act of writing the text or the written text (i.e., the autograph) itself. He is simply concerned to present it as a criterion which he believes accounts for the overall truthfulness of Christianity, as tested by the accuracy of biblical references in historical and archeological matters.

In Chapter XI of the *Apologetics,* Carnell considers the effects of higher and lower criticism upon traditional Christian theology in some detail.[174] The inerrant autographs best account for the confidence the Christian believer has in operating within a system which is both self-consistent and in full accord with life and experience. Lower criticism, defined as the activity of distinguishing earlier from later texts and manuscripts of Scripture and thus determining the nature and location of errors of transmission, is viewed as affirming this "high" view of the Bible. In fact, only the postulate of an inspired and inerrant autograph can account for the "objective science of criticism" and serve as a criterion or norm by which to separate erroneous copies from true ones. Since divine afflatus is the postulate that accounts for the propositional or doctrinal purity of the autographs, however, lower criticism is faced with the theological problem of why God would not extend this protective influence beyond the original authors to the copyists as well, thus ensuring the certainty of faith in the present.

Carnell gives several types of response to this problem: that God willed the situation; that perfect copies, like perfect autographs, might become the idolatrous objects of worship; and that the problem is analogous to the christological problem of Jesus being sinless but still being "broken by the blunderous actions of sinful men."[175] The most interesting type of response for our purposes, though, is the following:

> [Permitting] man to fall into transcriptional error in so holy and religious an assignment as copying the originally inspired manuscripts, is the highest possible testimony to that complete penetration into our inward lives that sin enjoys, and shows that, no matter how hard a zealot may concentrate, pray, and petition for grace, he still falls short of the immaculate Son of God. . . . Meditation upon the problem of transcriptional errors, therefore, ought to excite us to repentance, not to fleshly arrogance, for, if we are apt to sin in matters which demand

so peculiar a reverence and caution, how much more do we need grace to be preserved from falling into the hands of the evil one in daily life?[176]

Here we notice Carnell deliberately attempting to wrestle with the existence of errors in that Bible whose divine inspiration has been taken to entail inerrancy. His solution to this problem is that the recognition of biblical errors by the believer may itself prompt that religious response which is fundamental to all Christian activity and all Christian theology: repentance. The perception of errors in the Bible is thus compatible with Christian faith, a compatability which we have seen Warfield and Montgomery explicitly reject. In fact, not only is it compatible with Christian faith, but it may even serve as proximate cause of religious repentance.

The significance of this solution ought not be overstated. In fact, its tentativeness is signaled by Carnell himself in his succeeding paragraphs, where he reaffirms the "Princetonian" implication of the doctrine of God with respect to the autographs: "The Bible needed to be originally pure to be commensurate to the work of a pure God. . . . God could not be perfect and still sanction a revelation which claimed to be originally without error, but was not."[177] On the other hand, even this brief and tentative proposal is unexpected within an a priori theological approach. As we have seen for those theologians whose theological starting point is the doctrine of God, whose methodological approach is deductivist in nature, and whose understanding of the Bible is that it is necessary for salvation, the possibility of the Bible containing errors is nil precisely because of the philosophical incompatibility of God and error. And Carnell is just such a theologian.[178]

His account of inspiration, inerrancy, the autographs, and salvation, though, differs from those of his evangelical predecessors. Whereas they had utilized the autographs argument to minimize the significance of errors in present copies of the Bible, Carnell uses it to introduce the theological possibility of errors being useful in the activity of God leading persons to repentance. He follows the last sentence quoted with the observation that "this compulsion [of the doctrine of God entailing inerrant autographs] holds only for the original writings and not for the present text, for the purpose of the present is to lead men to repentance, and a document preserved substantially pure is sufficient to accomplish this task." Warfield's autographs argument has been turned on its head. Warfield included the autographs within his inspiration theory as a way to confer the authority of those autographs onto present translations of the Bible. As we have already noted, the presupposition behind this move is that errorlessness per se entails authority. Carnell, though, draws attention to the fact that it is the phenomenon of errors which precisely distinguishes copies from autographs. For him, error does not of necessity extinguish divine activity. Rather, it is the truth of the biblical message leading to repentance which is the locus of the Bible's authority. If the inerrant autographs are relevant, it is only because they are a part of the doctrine of God and *not* of the doctrines of anthropology and salvation which are the primary foci of the Bible in the present.

It cannot be substantiated that the early Carnell deliberately or intentionally set out to undermine the theological significance of the autographs, but he did do so. We have seen two ways in which this occurred. The first is through his insistence that the ultimate basis for deciding the truth or falsity of any proposition is a judgment of the mind concerning its "expectations" with respect to reality. Whatever he meant by this observation concerning the theory of knowledge, it is clear that he could not mean that judgments concerning truth and falsity are entirely passive. The judging mind brings something to the data which it judges, even if only the expectation that the law of contradiction cannot be broken. Because the mind which judges the truthfulness of biblical statements is likewise as active, it too cannot rest passively upon the unexamined assumption of inerrant statements. The mind brings an expectation to the reading of the Bible, and thus the concept of inspiration must reach outside the Bible to include an analysis of that expecting mind.

The second way in which Carnell weakens the evangelicals' dependence upon the autographs argument is by referring more to the dissimilarity of autographs and present copies than to their similarities, as earlier evangelicals had done. In making the distinction in this way, he draws attention to the possibility of inspiration applying to the present encounter of believers with the Bible, rather than being an exclusively past-oriented phenomenon referring to persons, words, or documents now departed. The *Apologetics* allows for the possibility of inspiration referring to contemporary insights which are awakened by and consonant with biblical insights, although this possibility is largely unexplored here.

It is fair to conclude that the early Carnell is an inconsistent deductivist theologian. Even at this point in his career, he evidences both conceptual and religious dissatisfaction with a theological method in which Christian faith is warranted strictly in terms of logical certainty. Admittedly, this dissatisfaction is not explicitly expressed; were the *Apologetics* his only writing, my interpretation might seem forced. On the other hand, given his laborious self-description as a rationalist and an a priori thinker, we are on Carnell's turf in noticing these systemic inconsistencies. Small though they may be, they give the attentive reader reason to suspect that the deductivist approach to Christian theology, especially that which is based upon the perfect autographs, is finally unable to account for an understanding of biblical inspiration. And this comes from one whose commitment to the deductivist approach is explicit.

Conclusion

The four theories considered in this chapter represent various points along a single spectrum. In simple terms, that spectrum is comprised of theories of inspiration which either ignore or neglect various factors involved in any act of inspiration. It has not been shown, nor would I claim, that these oversights were malicious in the sense of being deliberate attempts to deceive interested persons and communities. What has been claimed, though, is that the authors considered have in various ways commonly overlooked the possibility of examining nonreligious instances of inspiration in order to determine their potential for illuminating the phenomenon of biblical inspiration. Rather than beginning with the familiar and journeying to the unfamiliar, a genuinely inductive approach, these theorists begin with their understanding of the doctrine of God. This understanding is then joined with a particular anthropology which entails that all communication from God to persons be inerrant. The exemplar of this communication is variously portrayed as a prophet (Hodge), a secretary (Warfield), and a historian (Montgomery). Each of these ways assumes that inspiration is a concept according to which human beings are passive, whether as vehicles or as receivers.

If there is a single way to summarize my objection to deductivist theories, it is that they have not been shown to be theories of *inspiration*. As we shall see in Chapter 3, inspiration as a concept refers to the indirect influence which one agent exercises (sometimes unknowingly) within another agent's life. Beyond this, nothing can be specified in advance with respect to matters of truth and accuracy on the one hand or the degree of contribution by the inspired agent on the other.

Here it is appropriate to pause and reflect upon what the deductivists were up to in their distinctive manner of explaining biblical inspiration. What we saw clearly in Warfield may be said of the others as well: "the church doctrine of the Bible" is more concerned with how theologians said that the Bible was composed than with how the Bible inspires the church. Why is that? It should be noted that I am not pointing out once again that some who claimed to be inductivists were in fact deductivists. Rather, I am asking another kind of question entirely: why were those who were most insistent about the complete uniqueness of the Bible so willing to merge their ad hoc explanations of its origins with lengthy discussions of what tradition claimed about the Bible?

I can only suggest an answer to this question at this time, although we shall encounter the subject again in the final chapter. Unwittingly, most probably, these deductivists themselves have provided a response. In spending time discussing "the church doctrine of the Bible," they illustrated the closeness of the relationship between the church and the Bible. That is, they showed that the Bible launched the church and continues to launch it today. The church depends upon the Bible in a way that individuals, for example, do not. Individuals would and do continue to survive regardless of the existence of the Bible, but that cannot be said of the church. Thus, the church has an essential stake in accounting for the effects of the Bible within it both long ago and at present.

On the surface, the deductivists we have considered unanimously took inspiration to apply to the words of the Bible. But they left room below the surface for an understanding of inspiration which views the church rather than the Bible as its primary product.[179] Far from seeing the deductivists merely as methodologically inconsistent in their intention to treat the church doctrine of inspiration, perhaps we should interpret them instead as straining to put into words what their tradition could not admit: that the real effect of inspiration is the existence of the church as a community of believers rather than a peculiar configuration of words which itself is alleged to demonstrate divinity. This interpretation admittedly strains at gnats with respect to Hodge, Warfield, Montgomery, and Carnell. It does, nevertheless, make sense of what is otherwise anomalous in their works: the tenacity with which they attempted to explain what they insisted was inexplicable.

2

Inductivist Theories of Biblical Inspiration

The deductivist approach to inspiration surely represents the characteristic approach among evangelicals during the period of primary interest for this study. It is not, however, the only method employed by evangelicals. A minority of authors, using a different approach, introduced the possibility that the inspiration of the Bible could only be understood once nonreligious instances of inspiration were understood. This method is called inductivist because it begins with what is more surely known by the mind through experience and proceeds to inspect what is not yet known through comparison with the known. Unlike the deductivist approach, where the criteria which distinguish proper from improper judgments of experience are assumed to be impervious to revision precisely because they are not products of experience, inductivism's critical criteria intentionally reflect the actual experience of persons. These criteria thus become subject to revision both in theory and in practice. This does not signal a loss of religious certainty, however. In fact, a gain in the certainty of religious knowledge is acquired precisely to the degree that more data, rather than less, may contribute to understanding.

Inductivist evangelical theologians do not begin with an uninspected given in their analysis of inspiration as do their deductivist counterparts with the doctrine of God and the concept of an inerrant Bible. Instead, they begin the analysis of inspiration at a much more basic level. The three theologians considered in this chapter all take "biblical inspiration" to refer primarily to the effects which the Bible has among those persons who call it inspired. Only then do they attempt to account for how it is that the Bible may be taken as the vehicle of inspiration. Inspiration, that is, is taken to refer to an act of the mind which perceives a source of enhancement and enlightenment outside itself. This source may or may not be a mental entity itself. If it is not, however, one is licensed to continue to seek for the *source* of inspiration in another knowing agent.

Formally, the types of means through which some agents inspire others are irrelevant to the concept of inspiration. What is relevant, especially in contrast to deductivist theories of biblical inspiration, is that the two termini of inspiration are both known agents, and in addition that there is always a *means* of inspiration. The search for an adequate account of inspiration must begin with these agents. Because of the difficulties generated by deductivist accounts which begin with the inspiring agent (God), the inductivist approach begins with the more familiar agent, the person whose experience of God has been inspired by means of the Bible.

As in the previous chapter, I have chosen to address the following theologians because of the differences in how they employ the inductive approach. Augustus H. Strong calls attention to the faith of the inspired person as a datum which deductivists overlooked but which can scarcely be ignored if one intends to discover what *Christian* inspiration is. Bernard Ramm calls our attention to two theological activities, inspiration and "the internal witness of the Holy Spirit." Although he does not explicitly relate them, I shall. I shall further claim that the internal witness functions as a theory of inspiration in that it is a beginning account of how the mind grasps religious matters. Finally, William Abraham performs the long-awaited task of exploring an actual instance of human or personal inspiration in order to determine how one ought to expect biblical inspiration to function. Along the way, he also draws attention to the unconscious identification of divine inspiration and divine speaking, an identification which, he believes, accounts for why so many evangelicals believe that the Bible is inerrant. It will be seen that inductivism is generally more successful at illuminating the activity or process of inspiration than was deductivism. We shall take from inductivists what we can and then proceed to other resources to help us in continuing the task of identifying biblical inspiration. The inductivists studied here represent an advance over their deductivist counterparts, but there is still more to an adequate conception of inspiration than what they give us.

Augustus H. Strong

Augustus H. Strong (1836–1921) was professor of biblical theology at the Rochester Theological Seminary in Rochester, New York, and served as its president from 1872 to 1912. At the beginning of what remains one of the most comprehensive analyses of Strong's theology, Carl F. H. Henry notes that he has been called "one of the four most influential Baptist theological teachers of his period."[1] He is important for this particular study, however, because he is one of the first evangelicals to attempt to account for the inspiration of the Bible in internal rather than external categories. That is, at the very time during which the Princeton school was developing an account of inspiration which was "objective" in that it was taken to be true regardless of the faith perspective of the readers of the Bible, Strong was attempting just the opposite. He intended to demonstrate that it is in the minds of believers that inspiration should be located. God's participation in the inspiration of Scripture is thus to be discerned in categories which include rather than ignore whether persons have been inspired to faith through the Bible. We shall thus have to account both for Strong's theory of knowledge and more specifically for his theory of inspiration.

For Strong, as for Warfield and Montgomery, theology is a science. As *scientia,* however, it does not simplistically divide objects of knowledge into the two spheres of "facts" and "theory," as Warfield did with his doctrine of the absolute indefectibility of Scripture and as Montgomery did with his insistence that the Bible alone contains all facts and theories relevant for religious knowledge and certainty. Instead, theological knowledge is seen to rest upon the same type of "faith" as does physical science: "faith in our own existence, in the existence of a world objective and external to us, and in the existence of other persons than ourselves."[2] Faith, for both realms of knowledge, is "a cognitive act of the reason, and may be defined as certitude with respect to matters in which verification is impossible."[3] It is conditioned by affection or love. Just as aesthetic science presupposes the recognition of beauty which is "practically inseparable from a love for beauty," so too theological science presupposes the "power of recognizing God which is practically inseparable from a love for God."[4]

Having discussed the legitimacy of theology as a science—that it has the same rational foundation as any other systematic reflection upon knowledge—Strong continues by examining the capacity of the human mind to know God and thus to know the relationships which exist between God and the world. The most significant aspect of this discussion for our purposes is that he rejects the Kantian notion that "knowledge" refers not to what objectively exists but rather simply to whatever is within the knowing agent's senses and faculties. Strong responds by asserting that Kant's "forms of thought" (i.e., a priori judgments) are themselves facts of nature and are thus implicitly assumed by Kant as objectively existing. From this Strong concludes that "the mind reads its ideas, not *into* nature, but *in* nature. . . . [Human understanding functions] as discoverer of nature's laws, not as creator of them."[5] Human knowledge may, in principle, be certain of the existence of objects in the external world. But if so, it may also be certain of the relation these objects have with each other since the knowing intellect is one of the objects actually relating to others. Then, because we are made in God's image (i.e., since there are "important analogies" between the divine and human natures[6]), it is possible to know something of God's nature and of his relation to the world by analogy from our reflection upon human nature and its relation to the world. The direction of Strong's reasoning here is significant. He argues from the more certain to the less certain, from anthropology to theology. The certainty of Christian theology is for him not a given and unexamined datum: "We conclude that, in theology, we are . . . warranted in assuming that the laws of our thought are laws of God's thought, and that the results of normally conducted thinking with regard to God correspond to the objective reality."[7]

In thus optimistically estimating the possibility of human cognition to know certainly, even if not always with certainty warranted by evidence,[8] does Strong preclude the necessity of divine revelation? He does not. In fact, his understanding of the necessity and formal meaning of revelation is nearly identical with those of Hodge and Warfield: "Man's intellectual and moral nature requires, in order to preserve it from constant deterioration, and to ensure its moral growth and progress, an authoritative and helpful revelation of religious truth, of a higher and completer sort than any to which, in its present state of sin, it can attain by the use of its unaided powers."[9] Strong elaborates by pointing to the same elements that Warfield had noted: humans need an "external" revelation because of both cognitive finitude and sinful habitude. Certain questions cannot be answered by reason or intuition, and others are actively resisted by the will. Thus, "we need a special revelation of the merciful and helpful aspect of the divine nature."[10]

From the necessity of revelation we are brought to the consideration of inspiration. For Strong, as for the other inductivists this chapter treats, "inspiration" is the theological description of that activity of the human mind which is most susceptible to divine interaction. It is first and foremost, though, an act located in the mind, and it must be understood as such. Inspiration thus cannot be understood as an a priori scheme to which both human knowing and the Scriptures must be conformed.

Strong begins his treatment of inspiration[11] with its definition:

> Inspiration is that influence of the Spirit of God upon the minds of the Scripture writers which made their writings the record of a progressive divine revelation, sufficient, when taken together and interpreted by the same Spirit who inspired them, to lead every honest inquirer to Christ and to salvation.

There are striking differences between this definition and that of Warfield, for example. Both call inspiration an "influence" upon the biblical writers. Strong, though, understands inspiration to guarantee a "secure transmission of needed truth to the future"[12] so that the honest inquirer may have sufficient reason to decide, if in fact he or she does decide, that what the Bible witnesses to is actually what God reveals concerning Himself and His relation to the world. Warfield, on the other hand, sees the effect of inspiration not as being a witness to divine truth but as actually producing discernible characteristics which are themselves direct evidences of the divine presence, specifically errorlessness. Thus, his protestations notwithstanding, Warfield is not able to locate a genuine human participation in the writing of Scripture because his anthropology asserts what his inspiration theory denies: the universality of moral fallibility. Strong turns Warfield around by declaring that "all real knowledge has in it a divine element, and that we are possessed of complete consciousness only as we live, move and have our being in God."[13] What was bifurcated in Warfield is refocused in Strong. Inspiration has a wider and a narrower sense according to which all knowledge and biblical knowledge, respectively, are witnesses to the divine participation in the knowing act and mind.

Strong is also far more willing to allow for a theory of inspiration to arise from Scripture than were his Princeton contemporaries: "The chief proof of inspiration . . . must always be found in the internal characteristics of the Scriptures themselves, as these are disclosed to the sincere inquirer by the Holy Spirit."[14] Thus, however the effects of inspiration are explained as actually effecting a change in the hearts and minds of persons, they will accomplish this change only when Scripture is taken at "face value." It is only through this initial attitude of inquiring trust in the Bible that the Holy Spirit will be able to work, "awakening in us experiences similar to those which it describes, [thus testifying to] its divine origin."[15]

What is not said here is as significant as what is. Specifically, Strong does not say that a particular theory of the divine-human relationship must be included in one's theory of inspiration, as the deductivist approach in general requires. Inspiration is a category of interest only to the religious believer, for the question of the divine provenance of certain writings will only arise once those writings have proven themselves, at least initially, to be religiously transformative in that person's life. But then, since the believer's interest in inspiration follows upon his or her religious transformation, there is no need of addressing errors, problems, and difficulties as religious data. *For that person,* the Scriptures which are under such scrutiny are the very Scriptures which have already proven to be religiously significant.

Strong now discusses in more detail the nature of that divine-and-human product which is the Bible. Like Warfield, he describes it as an "equal" production of God and of persons, "therefore never to be regarded as merely human or merely divine."[16] He thus also understands it on analogy with the divine activity in regeneration and sanctification. Unlike Warfield, though, Strong takes the analogy between inspiration and sanctification as a genuine one.

Strong first denies that inspiration is properly conceived of as an "external impartation and reception."[17] In another place he writes that "man is not a mere tangent to God, capable of juxtaposition and contact with him, but of no interpenetration and indwelling of the divine Spirit."[18] Thus, far from natural abilities and fallibilities being overwhelmed by the process of inspiration, Strong seems rather to countenance the view that human nature is brought closer to its ideal expression when interpenetrated by the divine: "man is never more fully himself than when God works in and through him."[19] He follows this argument not just to the point of cultural and literary style, as had Warfield, but also to the point of scientific and historical errors.

Inspiration as a process is "dynamical" rather than "mechanical."[20] By this Strong means to say that every psychological phenomenon present within the knowing consciousness in nonreligious cognitive acts must be accounted for in religious cognitive acts as well.[21] This in turn means that the Scriptures cannot be said a priori to be errorless. Perhaps they do contain errors, but if so, then those errors are not located within the scope of those things concerning which the Scriptures have already been taken to be authoritative, that is, matters of "faith and practice."[22]

At first glance this appears to violate Strong's inductivism since it presumes that errors and authority are mutually exclusive. There are several ways to test this conclusion, the first being the way Carnell treated them. The second way, which we shall now consider in some detail, is that Strong introduces the principle of the "intention of Scripture" as a critical factor distinguishing legitimate from illegitimate[23] uses and analyses of the Bible. "Inspiration did not guarantee inerrancy in things not essential to the main purpose of Scripture. [It] went no further than to secure a trustworthy transmission by the sacred writers of the truth they were commissioned to deliver." He elaborates by saying flatly that "God can use imperfect means. . . . [As] God reveals himself in nature and history in spite of their shortcomings, so inspiration can accomplish its purpose through both writers and writings in some respects imperfect."[24] The purpose of Scripture must then be determined a posteriori, and it is that purpose realized in the lives of believers which is the effect of biblical inspiration.

The authority of Scripture is not to be located in the words of Scripture, as though they could have an authoritative status apart from their reception and appropriation by the believer. The authority of the words of the Bible cannot in fact be separated from the effect which they exercise in the life of the believing community, although these may be distinguished for heuristic purposes. But the effect of the words of the Bible is belief, that is to say, the appropriation of the Bible's witness to God's love for the world in Jesus Christ. For Strong, as for Luther, "the central subject and thought which binds all parts of the Bible together, and in the light of which they are to be interpreted, is the person and work of Jesus Christ."[25] As a hermeneutical key, however, the centrality of Jesus Christ in the Bible is a factor which will be relevant only to those who already understand and accept the message of Jesus in their lives as members of the believing community. That is, the hermeneutical significance of Christ must in the very nature of the case follow upon the religious perception of Jesus as constitutive of God's gracious act within the world and especially within the community of Christian faith. The authority of Scripture, then, is its indispensability in witnessing to the relationship which God establishes with the world through the Church. "While inspiration constitutes Scripture an authority more trustworthy than are individual reason or the creeds of the church, the only ultimate authority is Christ himself. . . . In thus judging Scripture and interpreting Scripture, we are not rationalists, but are rather believers in him who promised to be with us alway [sic] even unto the end of the world and to lead us by his Spirit into all the truth."[26] The authority of Scripture is thus a conditional authority. It is conditional upon the religious appropriation of its central message, a message which itself is taken by Christians to be a universal truth: God's love for and acceptance of the world as shown in Jesus the Christ.

It thus appears that Strong in part shares with Warfield an unwillingness to allow authority or normativity to coexist with error. That unwillingness led Warfield to reject error anywhere in the Bible, whereas it leads Strong to reject it only in those parts of the Bible which involve the intention of Scripture, that is, the religious significance of Jesus. In principle, though, the positions seem to be identical. In order to determine whether they are, we shall consider his treatment of biblical errors.

Having specified that the purpose of the Scriptures is incoherent if the faith of the believer is overlooked, we would expect Strong to discuss actual instances of the "imperfect means" of the Bible. Curiously though, especially in view of his insistence that the category of biblical errors must be relative to matters of faith and practice rather than to matters of science in its modern sense, he is most unwilling to admit of *any* errors in the Bible. He considers ten separate classes of alleged errors[27] and finds no justified indictment in any of them. Taking the class of historical errors as an example, we find Strong responding that present "errors" may result from fallible copyists, the "permissible use of round numbers," and the differing cultural and intentional perspectives of the writers. He finishes, though, by insisting once again that "inspiration is still consistent with much imperfection in historical detail and its narratives do not seem to be exempted from possibilities of error."[28]

This insistence upon the "actual" errorlessness of the Bible results from the convergence of two emphases and not from a third, as may be illustrated by examining Strong's terse dismissal of the apologetic importance of the autographs.[29] The two emphases which do inform Strong's conclusion concerning errors are, as we have seen, his specification of the purpose of Scripture as being soteriological and his insistence that God can and usually does work through fallible means to accomplish His will. What seems less warranted as explaining his unexpected conclusion about errors in the Bible is an incipient or recalcitrant a priori attitude concerning the doctrines of God and of Scripture. Strong makes his position clear in two brief paragraphs. In the first, he rejects the deductive argument from the doctrine of God. The argument is that a fallible Bible would not reflect appropriately upon the character of God, and Strong rejects it by noting that it "seems dominated by an a priori theory of inspiration, which blinds [it] to the actual facts of the Bible."

His second paragraph, though, is theologically more inventive. Here he says that the argument concerning the autographs presumes a causal relationship between inerrancy and authority such that if the former is not present, the latter could not in fact be exercised. The question he asks here is, in effect, why *this* causal relationship is the relevant one. Why should authority necessarily rest upon inerrancy? Elsewhere he argues that authority in both religious and nonreligious matters typically does not rest upon errorlessness. [30] Here, however, his position is more in accord with the approach which takes the authority of the Bible as being of interest only to the person who has already experienced it. With respect to this person, Strong asks rhetorically, "Does the present error destroy the inspiration of the Bible as we have it? No. Then why should the *original* error destroy the inspiration of the Bible, as it was first given?" This argument asserts that the authority of the Bible is grounded not in any objective person-independent qualities which may be said to belong to it, but rather in the fact that it has proved to be the proximate cause of a perception of human dignity and divine benevolence which positively reorients the person's life to itself. [31]

Strong does not reject the significance of the autographs argument on account of their irretrievability. [32] Nor does he reject it because it ignores the recognition that the *graphe* for which 2 Timothy 3:16 claims *theopneustos* were in fact some version of the Septuagint and were certainly not the autographs. [33] Rather, he rejects it because of its simple irrelevance to the concrete experience of the religious believers who recognize in the Bible both the formulation of and the response to questions which impinge upon them at the center of their lives but which they are unable to answer for themselves. To the believer whose Christian way of life has been structured by biblical narratives, metaphors, kerygmata, and confessions, the consideration of "errors" in that Bible is moot for all but explicitly intellectual purposes. In thus emphasizing the necessity of placing the matter of inspiration within the context of the exercise of religious belief, Strong illustrates the discovery of modern philosophy of language that "any attempt to analyze language of any sort apart from the user is doomed to inadequacy." [34] For Strong, the Bible's inspiration refers to the saving effect which it conveys to those to who are saved. No theory of inspiration need account for groups of persons outside of this one, it would seem, simply because no other group finds the Bible to be religiously inspired. As Hodge reminded us, theory need not go beyond facts.

Is Strong completely innocent of the charge of a recalcitrant a priori attitude concerning the compatibility of authority and errors? Probably not. We have seen that, unlike Warfield, he clearly asserts that no contradiction exists between them. And we have seen that the force of this assertion for Strong does not rest upon the autographs. However, we have also waited in vain for Strong to consider any actual error, regardless of how seemingly insignificant, even if only to show that it really is irrelevant to faith and practice. He does just the opposite and, like Hodge, affirms the possibility but not the actuality of errors in the Bible.

We are now able to address a final element in Strong's theory of inspiration, an element which is initially puzzling in view of his insistence upon the internal testimony of the Holy Spirit as that which finally "proves" the inspiration of the Bible. Strong writes that "miracles and prophecies" attest to the genuineness of both revelation and inspiration and that the modern believer might be strengthened in accepting both because of the evidential effects of those events: "A miracle is an event in nature, so extraordinary in itself . . . as fully to warrant the conviction, on the part of those who witness it, that God has wrought it with the design of certifying that this teacher or leader has been commissioned by Him."[35] Why this inclusion of external evidence within accounts of revelation and inspiration which are otherwise grounded on the internal phenomenon of personal faith?

It appears that this question is substantive and that Strong did perhaps retain elements of external verification within his inspiration theory. Miracles not only coincide with "purity of life and doctrine" to underscore the validity of a person's writing; they also at times "primarily and directly certify to the divine commission and authority of a religious teacher." When these three factors converge, they "mutually support each other, and form parts of one whole. . . . The authority of Christ as a teacher of supernatural truth rests upon his miracles, and especially upon the miracle of his resurrection."[36]

Because Strong is ambiguous concerning the status of externals such as miracles and prophecies as evidences which attest to and strengthen faith, rather than faith perceiving certain events as miraculous or prophetic, the reader alone is finally responsible for settling upon an interpretation of Strong which makes greatest sense out of the ambiguity.

Two avenues of approach are available to the interpreter who wishes to see continuity in Strong's theory. The first recognizes his acceptance of the coincidence of divine and natural activities in general. Divine activity may be discerned in all natural events, not solely in the extraordinary events of theophany, miracle, prophecy, and the like, since "natural law [is] the method of God's regular activity." God is immanent within nature, and His activity may be described as "immediate agency."[37] Extraordinary events may be clearer instances of God's purposive power at work, but they are not categorically distinct from other phenomena which believers accept as attestations of faith.[38] But neither are they distinct from the type of evidence accepted as sufficient for justifying beliefs in the natural or scientific realm since, as we saw earlier, science and theology are but two aspects of the same cognitive process. Miracle is not an intervention of God into the laws of nature. The perspective which believes that it is an intervention is unwarranted because God, as "principle of *all* growth and evolution,"[39] would thus be separated from the usual means used to accomplish His purposes in the world. Instead, miracle is an especially clear manifestation of the divine presence which is the condition of all proper thinking.[40]

The conclusion seems justified, then, that miracles attest the inspiration of the Bible, but not in a way that logically undercuts and overwhelms unbelief, which is the traditional way of thinking about miracles. Instead, *the* miracle which attests inspiration is the insight, mediated through the Bible, that God is copresent in all worldly events, including in particular the event of perceiving the Bible itself as the word of God.

The second avenue of approach is similar to one we have already noticed in Strong, namely, that the persons upon whom the attestation of miracles and prophecy is said to work are believing persons. That is, they are persons who already recognize and confess the existence of God and "who see in Christ none other than the immanent God manifested to creatures."[41] For such persons, conversion to Christian thinking means that Christ is taken to be creator, as well as redeemer, of the world. The centrality of Strong's christology is evident in the following passage:

> The second [person of the Trinity] is called the Word of God, and it is intimated that he constitutes the principle of objectification, consciousness, intelligence within the divine nature, and the principle of expression, manifestation, revelation, by which God is made known to other beings than himself. Christ, then, is the Reason, Wisdom and Power of God in exercise. . . . Since Christ is the principle of revelation in God, we may say that God never thought, said, or did anything except through Christ.[42]

The evidence which miracles and prophecy provide the believer, while "external" to the consideration of inspiration per se, is not external to that belief structure as a whole which sees Christ as the self-disclosure of God in granting salvation and in the operations of the world. "Miracle and prophecy" mean that God's transcendence is not restricted to the supernatural and the extraordinary, and that human beings may therefore become what they themselves cannot accomplish. Biblical inspiration refers in particular to the realization that the transcendent God is discerned as the ultimate source of the humanly authored biblical message.

We have seen that Strong's theory of inspiration is conditional upon faith; the assessment of the authority of the Scriptures cannot be independent of the acceptance or rejection of the message of the Scriptures. It is conditional as well in that Strong is unwilling to insist upon the structure of his theory as the only possible account of the importance of the Bible in the life of the believing community:

> Although we propose this . . . theory as one which best explains the Scripture facts, we do not regard this or any other theory as of essential importance. No theory of inspiration is necessary to Christian faith. . . . The fault of many past discussions of the subject is the assumption that God must adopt some particular method of inspiration, or secure an absolute perfection in detail in matters not essential to the religious teaching of Scripture. Perhaps the best theory of inspiration is to have no theory at all. [43]

Strong's modesty ought not be allowed to overshadow the attention he drew to the possibility of locating inspiration in primarily anthropological rather than primarily divine categories. For the first time among evangelicals, [44] the attempt is made to account for inspiration in terms of its effects among believers rather than in terms of the "divine status" of the biblical words themselves. This shift is not insignificant. Although Strong himself is frustratingly ambiguous concerning whether the Bible itself is error-free, he is useful to the evangelical community. The avenue is now open to viewing inspiration as a phenomenon which occurs within the actual course of natural and especially mental events, rather than as a phenomenon which absolutely restricts the operation of God to extraordinary and presumably divine effects. There are many ways in which God reveals Himself to human beings, writes Strong, but "the general method seems to have been such a divine quickening of man's powers that he discovers and expresses the truth for himself." [45]

Bernard Ramm

Bernard Ramm (born 1916) is a Baptist pastor, professor, and theologian. He has taught in a variety of Christian colleges and seminaries in the United States and abroad and has also been involved with such evangelical organizations as Young Life and World Vision. He has authored more than one hundred articles and nearly twenty books on topics including Christian education, ethics, exegesis, hermeneutics, apologetics, and fundamentalism. His most recent book explores the methodological differences between fundamentalism and evangelicalism. [46] The basic difference between them, he says, is that evangelicalism is open to the advances in critical understanding offered by the Enlightenment, whereas fundamentalism is not. This criterion, it may be seen, is very similar to the third one proposed in my Introduction.

Ramm is important to this study in that he, like Strong, views inspiration as a category of the mind rather than of the extraordinary qualities of a book. As we found with Strong, however, Ramm is ambiguous in presenting his understanding of inspiration. In several places, for example, he refers to the product of inspiration as the Scriptures themselves instead of as the interaction of the community with Scripture. We shall attempt to show, however, that Ramm describes inspiration differently from how he defines it. This description is of an activity which necessarily includes the reader's cognitive functions and is not restricted to evaluating the extraordinary qualities of the Bible. In particular, I shall claim that Ramm's account of "the internal testimony of the Spirit" is his description of how biblical inspiration functions and must therefore be accounted as part of his theory of inspiration.

Ramm's most detailed treatment of inspiration and revelation is found in *Special Revelation and the Word of God.*[47] Here inspiration is discussed as a subsidiary "product" of revelation, that is, as a phenomenon which lacks intelligibility when considered apart from revelation. Revelation in turn is described as that activity of God which brings "to the sinner a soteric [saving] knowledge of God."[48] This point is crucial to understanding Ramm. He expends a great deal of energy establishing it as the sole characteristic which distinguishes a proper understanding of revelation from illicit "bibliotry" on the one hand and "liberalism" on the other.[49] Revelation is that activity which both corresponds to and announces divine redemption: "Special revelation thus parallels . . . redemptive action, reports this redemption, and reflects upon it."[50] Unless revelation is thus seen as dependent upon redemption, it "appears as sheer didactic impartation of knowledge, and not as the word of life."[51] A theological as well as chronological ordering of these data, then, must place redemption before revelation, and revelation before inspiration.

What is the significance of inspiration? That is, what does it accomplish within the complex transaction of communicating a divine intention (human redemption) into an actual reality (human salvation)? Ramm notes that it has two functions. First, it has a "conserving" or preserving function in that "it seeks to continue revelation in an authentic form." Second, it has a "forming" function in that "it produces the specific document of special revelation, that is the *graphe.*"[52] Thus, "the function of inspiration [is] to preserve . . . revelation in the form of tradition and then in the form of a *graphe.*"[53] The latter citation is significant in that Ramm agrees that inspiration may apply to phenomena in addition to written documents alone, in this case the oral tradition from which the Scriptures were redacted. It is this attribution of inspiration to "other" phenomena which in part warrants the interpretation of Ramm that I shall develop below.

Ramm, as Warfield had done previously, refers to inspiration as a "concursive" activity. That is, a person who is inspired "speaks or writes without any consciousness of a divine afflatus. Yet the Holy Spirit moves along with the speaking and writing in such a manner that the thing spoken or written is also the word of God."[54] Elsewhere he calls concursive inspiration a "normal human activity."[55] He does not, however, mean what Warfield had meant by this term.

Warfield, it will be recalled, had so defined "concursus" as to remove from it any unambiguously human element, thus allowing it to stand for a divine-human activity in which there was nothing human. The net result, he assumed, was a product whose authority was as unquestioned as that of God Himself. Ramm restores both poles of concursus. He does so because of the violence done to the Scriptures when approached from Warfield's perspective. That perspective "flattens out" all reading of the Bible so that even the stylistic differences among the various authors become irrelevant:

> Much harm has been done to Scripture by those within and without the church by assuming that all statements in the Bible are on the same logical level, on which level they are either true or false. How untrue this is to oratory and literature! Oratory and literature move on several levels of communication and in and out of numerous universes of discourse, and with each change the problem of truth alters. . . . At this point *biblicism* and *criticism* can fail to come into proper focus. Biblicism may fail to see the literary character of Scripture and treat Scripture like a code book of theological ordinances. Criticism may be so preoccupied with the literary aspects of Scripture that it fails to see the substance of which literature happens to be the vehicle.[56]

Ramm affirms revelation as something spoken or written, thus susceptible to the same types of interpretation considered appropriate for all uses of language. Inspiration, thus, will likewise be understood in categories relevant to both spoken and written language.

Before developing the interpretation suggested above concerning Ramm's contribution to the doctrine of inspiration, it is necessary to discuss in more detail the "conserving" function of inspiration already mentioned.[57] Following Hans Engelland, he distinguishes among original revelation, oral remembrance, and written tradition,[58] with original revelation being correlative to the act of redemption. The conserving purpose of inspiration is to preserve the witness of divine redemption throughout these three successive stages of revelation in order to maintain its original content for readers of all generations. Oral tradition alone could not fulfill this purpose because of the propensity of the human mind both to forget and to distort. *"Only the written word could settle those issues controverted by willful or sinful men who would not abide by the oral word. . . . A written revelation came into existence because oral tradition as such could not sustain itself."*[59] How this preservation is accomplished Ramm does not say. In another place he settles for the traditional disclaimer that inspiration is not mechanical in the sense of dictation theories but that beyond that "Christian speculation" could not go.[60]

It would seem, though, that Ramm is not sufficiently faithful to his own emphases here. In denying the appropriateness of "speculation" concerning the operation of inspiration, he overlooks his insistence upon redemption and revelation as necessarily prior to inspiration. If "the function of revelation [is] to bring to the sinner a soteric knowledge of God,"[61] then the only persons who find the Scriptures to be inspired are those who are "saved," that is, those who accept the witness of redemption. The realization of Scriptures as inspired is necessarily consequent upon their having inspired someone. In the absence of that which the Scriptures inspire—divine salvation—logically there can be no inspiration to consider, since the appropriation of divine salvation is always prior to inspiration in the theological ordering of these doctrines. It would seem, then, that to consider the notion of biblical inspiration abstractly, as though it were intelligible apart from the reception of redemptive activity, is impossible.[62] But this is not a conclusion of mere "speculation." It is, instead, consonant with his doctrinal ordering of redemption, revelation, and inspiration, and also with Christian experience.

Enough has been said by this point to show that Ramm's understanding of the inspiration of the Bible necessarily includes reference to the believer whose salvation has been inspired by (or, more accurately, through) the Bible. Furthermore, this understanding is a recognition, not of the "divine qualities" of the Bible per se (whatever that would mean), but rather of the satisfactoriness of that to which the Bible witnesses as salvation from sin. "Inspiration" is thus a reflective term in the sense that it refers to a complex past experience: the experience of salvation in the present which is consonant with the salvation experienced by those persons and groups of persons portrayed in the Bible. It would, accordingly, be anomalous for persons to look for instances of where the Bible *is* inspired; rather, one looks for instances of where the Bible *has* inspired.

With respect to the notion of inspiration thus understood, the question now becomes how to describe the "process of transition" from an outlook not biblically inspired or shaped to one which is. How, that is, does Ramm suggest that inspiration inspires? It is here that I come to a conclusion that Ramm never explicitly drew but which is at once a sympathetic interpretation of him and also a significant contribution to an evangelical doctrine of biblical inspiration. In brief, what Ramm carefully explains as John Calvin's "internal testimony of the Holy Spirit," or the *testimonium,* is the functional equivalent of inspiration.[63]

Ramm begins his treatment of Calvin's doctrine of the *testimonium* by noting that the uncertainty of its derivation in Calvin does not obscure its soundness as a statement concerning "the source of the Christian's certainty that the Scriptures are the Word of God."[64] The location of this certainty is contrasted with three alternatives: the Roman Catholic notion[65] that certainty is bestowed by the church on the believer, the "enthusiastic" notion that certainty is granted by an immediate activity of God not grounded in Scripture, and the rationalist notion that religious certainty could be exhaustively tested by logic and reason.[66] In contrast, the *testimonium* is a work of the Holy Spirit in that it is a completed interior persuasion of the truth of matters concerning which the mind has no natural competency or interest. It is independent of Scripture per se, not in the sense of being opposed to the content of Scripture but rather in the sense of being an acceptance of those redemptive acts of God to which the Scriptures witness but which occurred in some cases long before the actual writing of Scripture: "Calvin's teaching that the *testimonium* existed before the Scriptures were written is fatal to the notion that for him the *testimonium* is sheer validation of Scripture apart from its content."[67]

An examination of some of the salient characteristics of the *testimonium*, interpreted now as "the functional equivalent" of inspiration, will help us to determine more precisely its contribution to an evangelical theory of biblical inspiration. It is first of all, says Ramm, a persuasion or illumination concerning information already received. As persuasion, it is a "form of influence directed toward free persons."[68] It is not an impartation of knowledge. It is the inward side of revelation and therefore can only function as there exists a given objective revelation. It would lose its character as a witness if it were an impartation of knowledge."[69] For example, the *testimonium* can establish neither the extent of the canon nor the resolution of textual variants within the canon, for both of these types of knowledge are "scientific" and are entirely external to the "inward character" of persuasion: "The persuasion is a persuasion to truthfulness. It is the simple, direct assent of the mind."[70] Once again, from a different perspective, we see Ramm's point that inspiration is unintelligible when considered apart from the appropriation of redemption.

Ramm also underscores the function of the *testimonium* as witness.[71] Two characteristics of the concept of witness are relevant to this study. The first is the usual meaning of witness which we may call the reflective meaning. Something which is said to testify, especially in a legal context, for example, reflects attention away from itself and onto an object. The adequacy of the witness is dependent upon the truth, the objectivity, the "settledness" of that other thing: "The witness and his testimony possess integrity only when the event in question actually occurred. Otherwise there is false witnessing." The second characteristic of the *testimonium* as witness is noted by Aristotle.[72] A witness not only refers to an event or fact as such but additionally is so convinced of its truthfulness that the witness intends to persuade others to believe as he or she believes. In other words, witnesses have convictions which they attempt to persuade others to adopt.

The notion of the inspiration of the Bible understood as witness or testimony is a significant development over the notion, common to a priori theories, which see it as guaranteeing the accuracy of a "record." In the latter class of theories, attention is drawn to the Bible itself as locus of characteristics which themselves constitute evidence of its divine origin. Here, for example, the Bible is uniquely specified as an inerrant book. One is then encouraged to read the Bible at least in part to encounter (and test) its inerrancy and thus its unique and divine specialness. When inspiration is understood in reflective or "witnessing" categories, however, attention is drawn away from the medium to the objective referent of the medium, in this case God's redemptive acts known in the present in the encounter of the mind with the message of the Bible. Rather than looking to the literary and logical characteristics of the book themselves as evidences of divinity, the reader reflects upon the salvation which he or she already possesses in virtue of having been internally awakened (or inspired) in the encounter with the biblical message. There is no danger of "subjectivism" here since the person is aware that the salvation inspired from within is not of his or her own making. More to the point, the opposite danger of making the appropriation of salvation wait upon tests for logical and literary consistency is also avoided.

As I stated earlier, if this interpretation of Ramm is valid then the process of inspiration may be described as a transition from an outlook not biblically shaped to one which is. "But how does a soul make the transition from comprehending the meaning of the sentences to a saving faith in the meaning of the sentences?"[73] Ramm's response is that the *testimonium* is what persuades a person of the truth of the Bible. In particular, one's persuasion is that "the content" of the Scriptures, that is, its central message, is the "saving relationship created between [Jesus Christ] and believing sinners through faith."[74] Ramm carefully distinguishes here between historical faith (for example, the belief that Jesus died on a cross) and saving faith (for example, that that death has redemptive significance *pro me* and *pro nobis*). The difference between these types of faith[75] is the effect of the internal witness of the Holy Spirit. The transition is not itself a property of the words of Scripture since, as in the examples just given, both types of faith rest upon those words. It is, rather, the persuasion of the saving significance of those words (and of that death) for one's life in the present. Thus, inspiration understood as the *testimonium* is not independent of the words of Scripture, but neither is it a property which applies exhaustively to those words.

Ramm takes as an example of "the transition" the Pauline declaration in 1 Corinthians 12:3 that "no one is able to say 'Jesus is Lord' except by the Holy Spirit." Here, he says, we see the transition made from a reference to a historical person to "an acknowledgment of his . . . divinity."[76] Conceptually, this acknowledgment "appears to be an impossible confusion of the temporal and the eternal, of the omnipresent and the local, of the infinite and the finite, of deity and humanity."[77] If, therefore, this acknowledgment or confession is made, it is made because it is seen as "the truth." Ramm does not specifically address what constitutes the truth or how it is known as the truth. However, it would seem fair to say here that the truth is that which a person accepts as unifying, or making sense of, previously disunified aspects of his or her life. For those persons who have experienced divine redemption in ways consonant with the experiences recorded and referred to in the New Testament, for example, redemption is redemption in Christ. Biblical inspiration thus summarizes the ways in which such persons refer to the indispensable role which the Bible has exercised in awakening that experience of redemption in Christ within them. The manner in which inspiration operates is similar to the manner in which any truth persuades the mind of its truthfulness.[78] Beyond this Ramm does not proceed; it is the Holy Spirit who is ultimately at work here, and the Spirit's actions are inscrutable.

It must be emphasized again that this is a deliberate interpretation of Bernard Ramm, indeed, one with which he may not agree. Evidence certainly exists that he might not:

> Nor can any specific notion of inspiration be gleaned from the *testimonium*. The witness of the Spirit illuminates the mind to the truth of the gospel, and to the divine authority of the documents which contain it. But it does not speak to the origin, mode of writing, or degree of inspiration. The persuasion is a persuasion to truthfulness. It is the simple, direct assent of the mind. But a special doctrine of inspiration would be a matter of knowledge and therefore would be out of keeping with the structure of the *testimonium*.[79]

Here Ramm clearly takes inspiration in its traditional sense as a property of the words and books of Scripture.

However, the question remains whether inspiration *should* apply solely to nonknowing and nonperceiving entities such as words and books. As noted earlier, Ramm's general description of a doctrine of inspiration is that inspiration is whatever is said to relate Scripture with revelation, that is, what relates the reading of the Bible with the personal appropriation of that saving activity to which the Bible bears witness. Ramm refers to this relationship as a type of persuasion, and likewise to the *testimonium* as a persuasion. Thus, my interpretation would seem to be a fair one. I do not deny that it is an interpretation, necessitated at least in part by Ramm's ambivalence concerning the description of inspiration. It is, in any event, an account of the impact which the Bible has had in the lives and minds of those persons who confess their salvation in Christian terms. As such, I believe, it constitutes "the functional equivalent" of a doctrine of inspiration.

William J. Abraham

William J. Abraham (born 1947) is a Methodist pastor and professor from Northern Ireland. He has been Lecturer in Philosophy of Religion and Christian Ethics at Queen's University in Belfast, and Assistant Professor of Theology at Seattle Pacific University. Currently he is professor of theology at Perkins School of Theology of Southern Methodist University.

Abraham's work on biblical inspiration[80] contributes to this essay in several significant ways. First, he stands within the Wesleyan tradition of evangelicalism, a tradition which has not yet been represented in this study.[81] Second, he not only refers to himself as an "inductivist," but intentionally analyzes nonreligious instances of inspiration in order to discover what light they might shed on the matter of scriptural inspiration. Third, Abraham takes seriously the distinction between revelation and inspiration, a distinction blurred by deductivists, as we have seen.[82] An important implication of this distinction is that, while the church no longer expects canonical revelation to occur, divine inspiration does occur in the present. Fourth, and perhaps most importantly, his method of inquiry is similar to the one I will develop in subsequent chapters, a method which is particularly appreciative of Thomas Aquinas.[83] We may thus hope to discover in Abraham an ally in the development of a theory of inspiration which is sensitive both to contemporary theological insights and to the broad tradition of evangelicalism.

The Divine Inspiration of Holy Scripture is a deliberate attempt both to criticize evangelical theories of biblical inspiration and "to offer a positive account of inspiration that is contemporary, coherent and credible. . . . My basic contention is that we can have a more adequate account of inspiration than that which became standard orthodoxy in the last generation."[84] Abraham's primary criticism of such theories is that they all[85] fail to take the concept of inspiration seriously. Instead, they depend, consciously or otherwise, upon the notion of divine speaking as the primary and often exclusive model of inspiration. The Old Testament prophet, the person who is alleged to have spoken exactly and only those words which God wished to have spoken, is taken as the paradigmatic illustration of inspiration.

Abraham rejects the identity of inspiration and speaking:

Any responsible and coherent account of inspiration must at least begin with the possibility that there is as much difference between divine inspiration and divine speaking as there is between human inspiration and human speaking. It must consider as a live option that divine inspiration is a basic act or activity of God that is not reducible to other divine acts or activity. It must not be confused with other activity of God, whether this be the creative activity of God or the speaking activity of God.[86]

As remedy for the problems generated by this identification,[87] and thus as starting point for an "adequate" theory of inspiration, Abraham suggests an analysis of the concept of inspiration as that term is used "in the common world of human agents. . . . [We] must first consider the word 'inspire' as it applies to human agents, if we are ever to understand it as it applied [sic] to God."[88] Thus, the reader expects Abraham to avoid "two fatal mistakes"[89] in the theory of inspiration which he constructs. The first is that of "beginning, continuing, and ending" with a doctrine of God, and the second is the reduction of inspiration to the mode of speaking.

Abraham takes as a "paradigm case of inspiration . . . a teacher inspiring his students."[90] The examination of such a case will reveal much about the concept of inspiration which will be useful in the attempt to understand divine inspiration specifically. Abraham first notes that inspiration is more a predicate of the student than of the teacher. That is, in any purported instance of inspiration, one's attention is first drawn to the person inspired and only then to the person inspiring and the mode of inspiration. Further, the natural differences among students lead one to anticipate a variety of "degrees of inspiration." The effects of an inspiring teacher will not be identical among all of that person's students. In addition, because students are active and not passive in the process of learning, their native intelligence and talent "will be greatly enhanced and enriched" as they experience the inspiring teacher. Natural faculties are in fact the object or intention of inspiration, and it is thus intrinsic to the notion of inspiration that there be positive enhancement of them.[91] With respect to the student, then, the final point is that inspiration itself is no guarantee of either complete accuracy or complete fidelity to the teacher. One thinks in this regard of the preface in a book, where the author acknowledges the positive influence of colleagues but dissociates them from any mistakes included in it.

Abraham next turns to the actual activity or mode of inspiration. He calls attention to the fact that inspiring is not done alongside other teaching activities but is rather accomplished "in, with and through" those other activities.[92] A farmer, for example, does not "farm" in addition to plowing, milking, planting, and harvesting. Rather, one who does these activities is farming. Thus, it is also the case that inspiration is quite often unintentional and even unconscious on the part of the teacher. What the teacher may consider quite routine, the students may find inspirational.

Finally, Abraham notes the effects of inspiration, especially that there is no single or sufficient indicator of its presence. Several "strands of evidence" must be present for an observer to conclude that a student has been inspired by the teacher. The foremost indicator, of course, is the testimony of the individual student. Other indicators may be "continuity of interests, outlook, and perhaps even style of approach to the issue at hand."[93] In the case of a group of inspired students, furthermore, a comparison of their work with that of their teacher will yield both similarities and dissimilarities. The similarity reflects the single source of their inspiration, while the dissimilarity reflects the original contributions of their learning faculties in interaction with what is communicated to them by their teacher. The degree of unity may not be specified in advance because inspiration is not mimicking. Nor may the degree of diversity be predicted, although Abraham does not say why.

His silence here is unfortunate, for it is precisely at the point of legitimate latitude or degree of difference that evangelicals have been especially perplexed. Precisely understood, though, we would argue that the question concerning the limits of diversity with respect to the meaning of inspiration is the same as whether a biblical writing or assertion may be considered inspired if it does not enhance one's understanding and experience of God. Seen in this light, the only available criterion for evaluating the limits of acceptable diversity is the practical or historical assessment of whether a particular narrative or assertion has in fact inspired the Christian community to (re)formulate understanding of the God-human relationship. If it has not so influenced the community, then it cannot claim to be inspired.[94]

Abraham next inspects the teacher-student paradigm to determine its appropriateness as an analogy for understanding divine inspiration. How far, in other words, does "the term [have] to be qualified when it is predicted of God"? Two qualifications are relevant here. The first and more important is that the paradigm is "highly intellectualistic," perhaps overly so. That is, it does not do full justice to the wide range of divine redemptive activities "through which God has inspired the writers of the Bible." The relationship between teacher and student is characteristically an informative or instructional one in which the student directly learns about a particular subject matter and only indirectly about the teacher. But not all acts of God are instructional in the sense of being communications of information. For example, Abraham notes that little if anything is learned about the character of God in the ongoing activity of the divine sustenance of the world outside of the fact that God "sustains" the world, a fact which one can learn perhaps even more directly from other sources. Nothing new is learned from reflecting upon "this" or "that" actual instance of divine sustenance. Yet the absence of a new datum of communicated information does not preclude the possibility of a person's being inspired (for example) to become more caring and considerate of others as a result of reflecting upon a given instance of God's sustaining the world. Inspiration is broader than strict communication of information.[95] It may occur along with the communication of information, but to identify the two activities is, strictly speaking, to confuse inspiration with revelation.

The second way in which the paradigm of instructional inspiration needs to be modified when used as an analogy for divine inspiration is not so much a qualification as a reminder that inspiration is not the straightforward enterprise that the deductivists took it to be. Instances of inspiration are difficult enough to justify in the case of teachers and students for reasons already noted, and additionally because not all students of a particular teacher will be inspired by him or her. With respect to God, though, who "is not an agent who can be located in the world of space and time," claims of inspiration will be vastly more complicated and thus even more difficult to certify. This reminder serves to underscore the similarity between divine and human instances of inspiration, and not to distinguish them.

The warning, though, is well heeded. The claim of a community to have been inspired by the Bible is initially a claim about the community's relationship with God and only then a claim about the Bible. Thus, the methodological attempt to understand such a claim must begin with the influence the Bible has had in that community; only then is it able to proceed to the question of the inspiring qualities of the Bible itself. A teacher who has not inspired students cannot be called an inspiring teacher, for without the effects there is no cause to consider. So, too, the attempt to understand the inspiration of the Bible begins with the inspection of a biblically inspired community.

Abraham believes that a significant correlative to his discussion of inspiration, in particular the distinction of inspiration and revelation, is that inspiration is not a divine activity strictly limited to the process of producing the Bible. Inspiration refers instead to a process in which one agent initiates an enhancing and enriching of another agent's knowing faculties: "Through his mighty acts of the past and through his continued activity in the present God continues to inspire his people."

It is only because of the confusion of inspiration and revelation that many evangelicals have attempted to account for the authority of Scripture with reference to inspiration rather than to revelation. The error of this account of authority is seen the more clearly that inspiration is seen as referring to enhancement and revelation as referring to content. When inspiration is understood exclusively by means of the model of speaking, the distinction between enhancement and content is blurred. When listening to a speaker, for example, it is extremely difficult to distinguish the impact of the speaker's message from the words used to create that impact; in this case, the spoken word is the heard word which creates the impact. Reflection on nonspeaking instances of inspiring, however, such as that brought about by painting, does allow us to distinguish them more clearly. Here, the medium of inspiration (the painting) is physically distanced from both the initiating agent and the receiving agent. The impact conveyed by the painting in the life of the viewer is more easily distinguished from the painting itself than is the impact conveyed by words from the words themselves. This is why we have seen Abraham reject the exclusivity of "speaking" as illustrative of the concept of inspiration. The inspiration of Scripture is discerned in the transformed life of the community, a transformation which Scripture mediates from God. It is only from within such a transformed community that it makes sense to discuss the means of inspiration as itself being inspired. Content will only be seen as inspired content by those who have been inspired by it.

Abraham's discussion is of immense practical help to the person who seeks to understand the function of inspiration rather than its abstract definition. He has made two significant contributions to this study. By calling to the reader's attention the unconscious identification of inspiration and divine speaking, he has clarified Ramm's warning not to confuse revelation and inspiration. As an agent, albeit a unique type of agent, God may inspire human beings in a speaking mode. He is not limited to the speaking mode, though, since not even human agents are thus limited. The figure of the prophet as God's spokesperson, therefore, is an appropriate model for the operation of divine inspiration, but it is scarcely the only one.

Second, Abraham's paradigm of teacher-student inspiration is extremely significant on at least two levels. As we have seen, the paradigm reminds us that the analysis of the concept of interpersonal inspiration begins at the level of the receiver of inspiration and only then moves to the levels of the initiator of inspiration and the modes of inspiring. Deductivist theories, while not identical, are uniform in their neglect of these categories. It is true that such theories begin by defining inspiration in terms of models which are consonant with Scripture.[96] They do not, however, take into consideration the experience of salvation undergone by all those who see the Bible as literary mediator of that salvation. As such, they reinforce the idea that biblical inspiration is an objective property of the words of the Bible which may be discerned by believer and unbeliever alike.[97] Abraham's analysis of the inspiration of students by teachers calls the deductivist approach to task for ignoring the significance of the faith in those persons and communities that claim to be inspired.

The other value contributed by the paradigm of teacher and student is found as much in its use in the first place as in any particular conclusion to be drawn from it. Abraham's choice of what we have called an interpersonal instance of inspiration is significant in itself. It signals a methodological approach which is, for the first time in all of the theologians we have considered, deliberately inductive in form. In beginning with the consideration of inspiration among humans and then proceeding to the consideration of the divine inspiration of humans by way of stripping from the human examples those elements not appropriate to the divine, Abraham neatly illustrates the approach of Thomas in the *Summa Theologiae,* I, 3, Introduction:

> Now we cannot know how God is, but only how he is not; we must therefore consider the ways in which God does not exist, rather than the ways in which he does. . . . The ways in which God does not exist will become apparent if we rule out from [the consideration of] him everything inappropriate [to him].

It is only those who already know God in some manner who can know the difference between appropriate and inappropriate statements concerning him. Both Thomas and Abraham presume in their very manner of approach that those who participate in their inquiries (concerning, respectively, the nature of God and religious language, and the nature of inspiration) already possess faith in God.[98] Without danger of oversimplification, therefore, we may say that the major distinction separating deductive from inductive conceptions of biblical inspiration is the recognition by the latter that the faith perspective of the person or the community is a necessary constituent in the concept of inspiration. The analysis of inspiration begins with those who have been inspired.

Abraham has contributed much to a concept of inspiration for consideration by evangelicals. He has not, however, completed the task as he led his readers to expect. In his introduction, for example, the reader is promised "an adequate account of inspiration."[99] And in his conclusion to the chapter on "The Concept of Inspiration" Abraham says, "In the course of this chapter I have attempted to provide and defend a positive account of divine inspiration. If the substance of this analysis is correct, then a coherent and serviceable doctrine has been furnished for the contemporary theologian."[100] It is my contention that Abraham has begun, but not completed, this task. In particular, what he has failed to provide is an account of the *divine* inspiration of Scripture. That is, he has said that God inspires the Christian community to salvation by means of the Bible, but he has not shown how God does that or how the community knows that it is God who ultimately initiates the salvation. In the final chapters of this book, I shall address these questions.

Abraham's enduring contribution is that the discussion of inspiration must begin by accounting for the act of personal consciousness that *accepts* the biblical message. Responses which locate inspiration exclusively in the Bible's words rather than in the act of consciousness which grasps those words are hopelessly incoherent because they neglect the most important constituent in the entire discussion: the faith of the community in which persons have been saved. There is no biblical inspiration where there is no faith inspired by the Bible.

Conclusion

At the conclusion of Chapter 1, it was noted that deductivist accounts of inspiration uniformly avoided being accounts of inspiration. Instead I noted that they were ad hoc accounts of the "extraordinary status" of the words of the Bible which were uncritically grounded in the doctrine of God.[101] This chapter introduced us to a second weakness of deductivist approaches, which is that they neglect to see the tripartite structure of the concept of inspiration. The three categories of this concept are, in Abraham's terms, the inspiring agent, the means of inspiration, and the inspired agent. Deductivist theories either fail to see these three categories or at best conflate the second and third, in their restriction of biblical inspiration to the words and authors of Scripture.

In different ways, Strong, Ramm, and Abraham have each encouraged us to begin the account of inspiration in the third category. They have thereby shifted our attention to that aspect of inspiration which has the greatest conceptual potential precisely because it is one with which we are more familiar. Strong reminded us that theology is ultimately grounded in faith, which is certitude that cannot be exhaustively verified but is not thereby illicit. Ramm's work brought to light the similarity between inspiration and persuasion, a similarity which confirms our belief that biblical inspiration ought not be seen as an ad hoc explanation of a unique activity. Finally, Abraham specified the three aspects of the activity of inspiration and showed that it is moot to discuss whether the Bible is inspired without first determining whether and how the Christian community has been inspired by it.

Two comments will conclude my survey of inspiration theories and launch an attempt at one. The first comment makes clear what has until this point only been implicit. In challenging the adequacy and coherence of theories of inspiration which assume that inspiration is located in the words of the Bible rather than in the lives of believers, we are challenging the meaning of the concept of inspiration as that meaning has been understood in most of Jewish and Christian tradition. That is, the confession that the Bible is inspired has traditionally been taken to mean that the uniqueness of the Bible could be entirely explained by examining the Bible itself rather than by examining the effect that it mediates to the believing community. Thus far in this book, I have questioned the adequacy of this traditional explanation. In so doing, I recognize the significance of my critical endeavor; I have called to task nearly every theologian, evangelical or not, who has thought and written about biblical inspiration in the last several thousand years. Although no defense may be able to overcome such hubris, it should at least be noted that I am aware of the scope of my critique. At this stage in my argument, then, not yet having begun to offer my own systematic reflections on inspiration, I can only trust that the criticisms I have made will justify the need for a significantly revised theory of biblical inspiration.

The second comment is that in making these criticisms, it is obvious that there is a difference between one's account of inspiration and one's experience of inspiration. And it seems equally obvious that these theories served as adequate models of the experience of biblical inspiration which many generations of evangelical Christians underwent, regardless of the conceptual difficulties inhering in them. That is, something in these accounts "rang true" in the lives of believers so that they were enabled to reflect clearly and adequately upon their encounter with God in their encounter with the Bible. Our next chapters will attempt to lay bare precisely what these theories were intending to say about God, the Bible, and the experience of God mediated by the Bible. Thus, the focus of critical activity will shift from what was "said" to what was "meant."

3

Inspiration and the Human Recipient

In the remaining chapters I will attempt to bring to light various insights which I believe should be included in a theory of biblical inspiration. To be successful, my theory must meet two discrete sets of criteria: those which distinguish responsible biblical scholarship on the one hand and those which distinguish evangelicalism on the other. Thus, not only will I have to avoid the pitfalls into which others have stumbled, but in addition I shall have to say clearly how it is that my theory fits in the evangelical community.

Accepting the tripartite structure of the concept of inspiration articulated by Abraham, I will first consider those aspects of inspiration which focus upon the receiving agent. Here I will reflect upon methodology, anthropology, and then the activity of the mind in inspiration. In the next chapter, we shall turn to the Bible as the medium of divine inspiration, paying particular attention to the discussions of verbal inspiration, plenary inspiration, and inerrancy. It is here that my intention to contribute to the evangelical community will be most apparent, because I will rework these characteristic evangelical concerns so that they are not susceptible to the criticisms made against them in earlier parts of this study. Finally, the last chapter will consider God, the initiator of salvation and inspiration. Here we will benefit in particular from the discussion of God carried on by contemporary Thomists to which William Abraham previously alluded.

Interest in Methodology

No reader of evangelical theories of inspiration can fail to notice the careful attention given to methodological issues. For each theologian treated in this book, the consideration of form or manner of approach has been obvious. To many persons, but perhaps especially to conservative Protestant Christians, such attention may appear to be misplaced. Probably the most representative reason for this suspicion is that methodological considerations are abstract and seemingly far removed from the ordinary exercise of faith. Thus, they would be of interest only to the specialist and not at all to the ordinary believer. The task in these next few pages will accordingly be to discuss the relevance and necessity of methodology.

We saw earlier that Hodge and Warfield fully believed that their theories of inspiration were inductive, but critical reflection upon their works indicates just the opposite. Montgomery, also a deductivist, would have his readers accept the truthfulness of the entire Bible on the grounds that "Christ was God" and that *He* affirmed that truthfulness. We could expand this analysis to apply to each theologian, of course, but the issue underlying all of them would remain the same: why were they so insistent that their works be of a particular formal structure? What is the *theological* significance of a method of approach?

The most straightforward response has to do, it seems, with the related notions of intelligibility and communicability. The way that one presents the concept of inspiration is crucial to an audience's understanding of its meaning, as redaction criticism has discovered with respect to the meaning of gospel stories.[1] What is presented poorly is likely to be understood poorly. In paying close attention to the form of presentation, the evangelicals emphasized that inspiration is of sufficient theological importance that it must not be inappropriately articulated lest it be misunderstood.

This observation seems painfully obvious and perhaps even trite. All that is obvious, however, is the general point that form as well as material conveys meaning. What is not so obvious, and why I believe that the evangelicals belabored the point, is that the same holds true for inspiration theory in particular. It has already been noted in this study that inspiration waned as a topic of theological interest to Protestants in the nineteenth and twentieth centuries. William Abraham illustrates this tendency when he says that "it is not disrespectful to say that what Professor John Macquarrie has written on [inspiration] in his widely used *Principles of Christian Theology* [SCM, London, 1966] could be put on a postcard."[2] The evangelicals' interest in inspiration, represented by the energy they expended in communicating it in deliberately chosen methodological form, indicates their commitment to retaining it as an item of continuing theological value.

There is more to the question of methodology than just the survival of inspiration talk. In addition, there is the matter of verification. Just as that which is presented poorly will be understood poorly, so too that which is presented chaotically cannot easily be verified or checked. This is precisely why evangelicals were so insistent that their methods be the methods which had already proven so astoundingly successful in the natural sciences. (This is no doubt why Hodge and Warfield used the language of inductivism to refer to their deductivist methodologies.) The evangelicals, as is evident particularly in Hodge and Montgomery, wished to show that they were simply returning to the approach of Scripture, a move which had not only the salutary effect of authenticating their particular efforts but also the entire inductivist apparatus of modern natural science.[3] Critical inductivism proceeds by a double movement from the known to the unknown and back to the known, with the second movement constituting the verification of the first. In theology, this double movement proceeds in the same way, with the known varying relative to what is accepted as bedrock certainty. Whether the starting point be "biblical fact" (deductivism) or "Christian experience" (inductivism), however, it is significant that both approaches see verification procedures as an integral part of inspiration theory. As interior as the work of inspiration may be, evangelicals do not accept it as a private act.

One's interest in methodology thus has great significance for one's theory of inspiration. Evangelicals in particular are sensitive to methodology for two more reasons. First, they wished to preserve the importance of the notion of inspiration at a time when their nonevangelical counterparts were characteristically abandoning it. (Why they were interested in preserving it will be discussed shortly.) Second, they wished not only to preserve it but to preserve it in such a way as to make it more understandable. Implicit in this effort is the criticism that the nonevangelicals had too quickly abandoned inspiration talk. Thus, they turned to that option which had so successfully expanded human knowledge of the natural world and coaxed it into use for theological purposes.[4]

Even a cursory acquaintance with evangelicalism in the present underscores the success of this course of action. For better or for worse, few subjects are as closely associated with evangelicalism as biblical inspiration and related topics. This is true not only for John Warwick Montgomery, Francis Schaeffer, Harold Lindsell, and others who call inspiration the watershed of contemporary evangelicalism,[5] but also for those evangelicals who are more temperate concerning the relative importance of inspiration talk,[6] such as Anthony Thiselton and Gerald Sheppard, whose specializations are philosophical theology and Old Testament respectively.[7] Careful attention to methodology has resulted in the cautious acceptance by many evangelical theologians of historical criticism with the intent of illustrating and illuminating the Christian tradition for use ultimately in pastoral and liturgical contexts, and never merely for historical and intellectual purposes alone.

If this interpretation of evangelicalism is correct, then we have discovered the major reason why evangelicals have traditionally been tardy in appropriating critical tools: it is because of their intent to make Christian faith communicable to the widest possible number of believers in both academic and worshiping contexts. Evangelical pastors and theologians have had to juggle several levels of interest simultaneously, such as remaining faithful to the text and tradition of Christian theology and history, becoming acquainted with critical tools and their use in matters theological, and meeting the personal interests and sensitivities of the believing audience in the classroom and in the pew. Inevitably, adeptness at such a complex task matures slowly. The point of special interest to this study, however, is that the task has been accepted by evangelicals. Inspiration talk has both survived and matured as a result of its deliberate coordination with the results of critical reflection upon the origin and meaning of biblical texts.

Basic Anthropology

The next two topics are closely related and in fact are distinguished only for the sake of discussion. In the present section I shall summarize the anthropology which I believe is characteristic of most evangelical analyses. In the following section I shall consider "the doctrine of the mind," or the implications of evangelical anthropological discussions with specific reference to the activity and passivity of the human mind in the matter of coming to know God. In both sections it should be kept in mind that I am not attempting a comprehensive survey of either topic. This study assumes that evangelicalism is irreducibly transdenominational or pluralistic. There simply is no single or unified anthropology to which all evangelicals in various denominations would subscribe. My effort, therefore, will be to present an anthropology with which many evangelicals would agree, not for the sake of evaluating the presentation itself but rather for the sake of going "behind" it to uncover its point or message. To borrow an analogy from Ludwig Wittgenstein, this summary discussion of anthropology will serve as a ladder for gaining access to the theological presuppositions of anthropology. Once we have gained such access, we will occupy a more advantageous perspective from which to suggest what a contemporary evangelical theory of biblical inspiration should say about the theological status of human beings.

I believe that there are three subjects to which all evangelical anthropologies both refer and return: that persons are creatures of God, that persons are created in the image of God, and that persons are selfish or rebellious creatures who are ultimately incapable of renewing the fractured bond or covenant between themselves and God.

To say that human beings are creatures of God does not distinctively characterize them, for if this is true of any part of the universe, then it is true of all parts of it. Nor is it consonant with only one cosmogony, as Charles Hodge reminds us.[8] Instead, it is ultimately a claim which situates human beings both vertically and horizontally.[9] Vertically, the claim asserts that no anthropology is complete which omits consideration of the relation of persons to God. Or, put more positively and more technically, talk of human beings transcendentally includes talk of God as the Being with whom all persons are constitutively related and on whom they always depend.[10] This claim is transcendental in that, while it cannot be empirically tested or demonstrated, its truth is taken by the Christian community (past and present) as a condition of the possibility of meaningful discourse about persons and the universe. Theologically, cosmogonic discussions are restricted only in that they must allow for scientists and theologians to integrate the "how" of this relation within the discussion; the only such discussion which is in principle invalid is the one which a priori excludes the validity of God language as a part of it.

The claim that persons are creatures of God also affirms the horizontal significance of persons in creation, namely, that to a great extent human beings are one with the rest of creation. If the vertical relationship has traditionally been overemphasized by evangelicals, this one has characteristically been underemphasized. That "God made human beings out of the [same] dust of the ground" as He made all other sentient beings not only affirms the material significance of human life (as compared to all platonizing schemes which denigrate the bodily and material), but additionally licenses in principle the analogy between conscious and self-conscious beings[11] which has been the basis of so much medical and anthropological progress in recent centuries.[12] Once again, the point of reflecting upon the horizontal implications of creature language for our purposes is to notice that the continuity of all sentient life, regardless of whether that continuity is argued from evolutionary or creationist bases, licenses what we have called the inductive approach to inspiration. In principle, at least, all of life is latent with instances which may serve analogously to exemplify the ways in which God inspires persons to a certain vision of life by means of the Bible. And conversely, because God is the creator of "all things visible and invisible," there is literally no limit to what He may use to inspire or bring about that vision of life. William Abraham is on good evangelical ground indeed when he illustrates biblical inspiration with the analogy of teacher-student inspiration.

What distinguishes human beings from all other conscious beings in the universe thus is not their status as creatures. Rather, it is their status as creatures in the image of God. The precise meaning of *imago Dei* is much debated, of course, but at root I would argue that it is the same as what anthropologists and philosophers refer to when they speak of human beings as self-conscious. To be self-conscious means not only that one knows but also that one has the ability to reflect upon one's knowing. Thus, self-consciousness is primarily a category of the mind in that it is an act of knowing. Only humans are able to objectify experience so that it becomes a datum of reflective knowledge which does not remain simply as a datum of passing experience. Many conscious creatures have the ability to think, but only persons are able to think about thinking.

It must not be assumed, however, that "the image of God" is exclusively an intellectual matter. It is also a moral or normative matter. In fact, it may easily be seen that the normative aspect is the condition for all reflective acts of consciousness. As such, it constitutes the more important constituent of the discussion of the image of God.

I have said that it is distinctive of human beings that they are able to think about thinking, that is, that they are able to make knowing itself into an object of knowledge. The reason that this is distinctive rather than coincidental to the present discussion is that persons are thus able to compare various bits of knowledge with each other in order to sift better ones from worse ones. This presupposes the ability to choose between good and bad. It cannot be claimed that the mere ability to choose is distinctively human; after all, even my cat exercises a choice when faced with a bowl of sardines on one side and a bowl of dry food on the other. What is distinctive is that humans objectify bits of knowledge and reflectively choose between them in such a way as to be able to articulate the reasons behind the choices for and against. That is, humans are able to distinguish right from wrong in principle, and not just between better and worse in the present moment. The human ability both to objectify and to evaluate bits of knowledge constitutes the foundational distinction between conscious and self-conscious beings and thus constitutes, I would claim, the meaning of "image of God." While both elements are necessary, the normative is seen to be more fundamental because it is the condition for the possibility of judging among abstracted and objectified bits of knowledge.

We are now in a position to consider the final subject contained within all evangelical anthropological discussions, that of human rebellion or sin. We have seen that the ability to make normative judgments is distinctive of human beings. We now must account for why these judgments and the practical decisions stemming from them so consistently assume a pattern better characterized by "sin" than by "fidelity" and then account for the relationship between anthropology and biblical inspiration.

Human beings have the ability to make normative judgments with respect to experiences which, when reflected upon, become objective bits of knowledge. Because such judgments are normative, humans are responsible for making them and so are responsible for the consequences of making them. But responsibility is a concept which presumes a condition of genuine moral freedom, since one cannot be held responsible for what one cannot avoid doing. Thus, just as the normative or moral capability of self-consciousness is the condition for evaluating among objectified bits of knowledge, so too, freedom is the condition for being responsible to decide and for the decisions made. The ultimate moral environment in which persons exist, therefore, is freedom. Or, to say the same thing from another perspective, a being is not a human being if it is not ultimately free to make normative judgments concerning its life *and* if it is not responsible to do so.[13]

Only human beings are able and responsible to make judgments concerning moral truth and falsity. The "doctrine of sin" simply intends to reflect human experience by concluding that persons characteristically judge falsely when faced with this responsibility. But false with respect to what standard or criterion? Evangelicals have answered this question by saying that persons judge falsely when they decide (i.e., when they believe and act) as though they and their desires were the ultimate measure of rectitude in the world. Because persons are both creatures of God and creatures in God's image they are unable to be such an ultimate measure and in fact are unable even to make a responsible judgment without implicitly affirming their moral inferiority vis-à-vis God.[14] But this does not preclude the attempt, and it is the attempt to be ultimately self-serving that is called sin against God.

Sin thus primarily refers to an attitude of ultimate, if not also immediate, self-sufficiency in considering and making judgments concerning human experiences. In more traditionally religious terms, sin is the human refusal to integrate one's dependency relationship with God into all of one's thinking and acting. Because sin refers to a fractured bond or covenant between God and humans, and because the fracturing is always initiated by humans and never by God, it may also be referred to as rebellion against God. In fact, "rebellion" seems to be a better metaphor here because it is more clearly a dynamic concept and also because it calls attention to the asymmetricality of the God-human bond: God always initiates, and humans always respond to that divine initiation.[15] The "deceitfulness of sin," to use the pungent phrase of Hebrews 3:13, may be seen to be precisely the human response of selfishness in the face of God's perpetual nonselfish giving of Himself to humans in and through His creation.

Although this analysis is almost painfully brief, it is, I believe, an adequate summary of evangelical anthropology. But what has it to do with biblical inspiration? What is the point of the discussion of creatureliness and sin with respect to biblical inspiration, a doctrine considered otiose by many Christian theologians? My response is that apart from such an anthropological analysis there is no proper foundation for any discussion of the inspiration of the Bible. I shall defend this claim with reference both to what has just been said about the God-human bond and to what has traditionally been called the formal principle of Protestantism.

As has been noted, the God-human bond is asymmetrical in that God is always seen as creator and therefore initiator, while humans are always seen as creatures and therefore respondents. Although this structure is taken to be constitutively true,[16] it is particularly descriptive of the situation in which persons use their freedom and responsibility in morally sinful or selfish ways. Under these conditions, if persons are to enjoy a proper relationship with God, it will only be because God initiates the healing (or *soteria*) of the fractured bond. Rebels qua rebels cannot overcome the conditions of enmity which they have introduced; it is only by means of genuine pardon and forgiveness on the part of the superior that those conditions may be returned to normalcy. The implication of human helplessness with respect to the doctrine of biblical inspiration is thus that it is in the Bible that persons encounter narratives of the acts of God which they recognize as sufficient to heal the breach which their rebellion caused in their bond with God. In reading and reflecting upon the accounts of people and of God in the Bible, persons are inspired (that is, they come to an awareness which they recognize is not of their own making) to understand the sufficiency of the character of God in overcoming and healing the fractured bond.

It is thus consonant with an evangelical anthropology that God is seen as "perpetual initiator" in the activity of overcoming the effects of human moral rebellion against Him. This is, I believe, precisely what is meant by the so-called formal principle of Protestant theology. First enunciated in the sixteenth century by Martin Luther, it asserts that "Scripture as illuminated by the Holy Spirit, is the only trustworthy guide in moral and spiritual matters."[17] On historical grounds it is clear that Luther intended this principle to apply specifically against the medieval Roman Catholic doctrine that the church was equally authoritative with Scripture, especially with respect to matters where the latter was silent. But the significance of this principle extends beyond its usefulness to a discussion by various factions in the medieval church. Fundamentally, the principle asserts that it is only the divine initiation in the reading or interpretation of Scripture that warrants its complete trustworthiness in religious matters ("Scripture *as illuminated by the Holy Spirit . . .*"). It has too often been assumed that the principle is a statement about the divine status of the Bible per se rather than about the interpretation of the Bible by present-day readers. This misunderstanding led directly to the excesses attributed (often correctly) to fundamentalists and evangelicals who sought evidences of inspiration in the very words of the Bible rather than in the encounter of the person with those words (i.e., their interpretation prompted or inspired by the Holy Spirit). But this is not what Luther meant. Even more importantly for our purposes, it is not what is at issue within contemporary evangelicalism. The point of interest at present is rather that God initiates the healing of the fractured bond between Himself and human beings.

A final point must be made concerning the specific relationship of anthropology to inspiration. Persons are creatures in God's image; they constitutively know the difference between truth and falsity at the very moment when they rebelliously strive to affirm the false. But because this is a constitutive knowledge, they also know the truth. Thus, the formal principle of Scripture also asserts that it is in the Bible that persons encounter the clearest expression of the truth concerning themselves and God. But how could this be so since those who wrote and compiled the Bible were rebels as well? Apart from some variant of the discredited dictation theory, why should it be assumed that what those persons wrote is any more transparent of the character of God (i.e., religiously authoritative) than what any other person may have written about Him?

My response to this question is that it is proper but typically misconstrued. Responses to this question usually focus upon characteristics of the Bible themselves as providing evidences of its divine authority. This study has already surveyed several possible characteristics. But what seems more promising as an avenue of response is the exploration of how persons have actually been inspired to a new understanding of God by means of the Bible. In that act (or, more properly, those acts) of inspiration, was their attention drawn to God as the initiating agent, to the authors of the Bible as the means of His initiating, or to the mere words of the Bible independent of their saving effects in their lives? Evangelical Christianity has long insisted that salvation (or healing) occurs when the bond between God and persons is restored and that the authority of the biblical authors and the biblical words lies solely in their witness to the sufficiency of God's actions to that end.[18] What is authoritative about the Bible is its indispensableness in serving as the medium of God's initiation as witnessed to by persons who have been inspired through it. Or, to say the same thing, "the inspiration of the Bible" at root is an abbreviated confession that a community has been inspired to a renewed bond with the God to whom the Bible bears witness and who uses that biblical witness as His primary means of inspiring that community.

To return to the question at hand, then, on theological grounds it may be seen that, strictly speaking, the character of the biblical author is irrelevant to the understanding of biblical inspiration; surely such persons were rebellious creatures, as our anthropology insists with respect to all persons. What is relevant is that the present community of Christian believers has been inspired to its understanding of God through, and not by, the biblical authors. That they were sinners is a given. That their words as handed down to us in the present are the words through which we are inspired to know God is also a given. Those words are inspired first because they reflect upon the experience of salvation inspired by God within the community of faith of the author, and second because they have inspired the Jewish and Christian communities to faith in God throughout the course of the centuries. But that in no way entails that they be "divine" or possess discernibly divine characteristics in addition. It is enough that, through them, we have come to know God as Savior and as the Father of Jesus.[19]

We have seen that the evangelical anthropology summarized here is correlative to a certain understanding of biblical inspiration. The anthropological analysis asserts that persons are capable of knowing the truth and in fact that they do know the truth because they are responsible for knowing it. Our understanding of inspiration is consonant with this anthropology. Because even rebellious humans may recognize the truth about themselves and God, the doctrine of inspiration being developed here asserts that that is precisely what occurs in the reading of the Bible. In that reading, a community recognizes the voice or word of God addressed to it and recognizes that voice or word as speaking the truth about it in ways which it is ultimately incapable of originating. Thus, the phenomenon of biblical inspiration, as all other instances of inspiration, is one of recognition, enhancement, and response to a mediated message.

The Activity of the Mind and Biblical Inspiration

The preceding section outlined a basic evangelical anthropology, an anthropology that is consonant with the experience of biblical inspiration which, I believe, serves as the initial and most certain experience of God for evangelical Christians. In this section we turn our attention specifically to the implications of that anthropology which bear upon the acts of the mind. How does the human mind function when it is inspired? Is it active, passive, or some combination of the two? What, if anything, does the mind contribute to the situation in which it is enhanced and thus enabled to appropriate an understanding of God which it accepts as a saving understanding of God? This question is, of course, the very traditional one concerning the psychology of inspiration, but from an entirely different perspective.

It is important to note that this question is not whether the human mind is able to know God. This is a most legitimate question, and it has received intense scrutiny, especially since the Enlightenment. It has not, however, troubled evangelicals.[20] Evangelicals have characteristically presumed a positive response here and have instead focused their attention on how to conceptualize and explain the meeting of the divine and human minds. In short, their interest has centered on "how" rather than "whether."

I believe that the human mind is both passive and active in the complex event called inspiration. This is in accord both with the anthropological analysis just presented and with the nonreligious paradigm of inspiration given by William Abraham above. In what follows, I shall attempt to account in an initial way for this claim, concentrating on how the believing mind functions when it encounters the witness of the Bible concerning God. This analysis cannot but be somewhat abstract, since it attempts to account for how inspiration works in general rather than specifically for concrete individuals. Furthermore, it is an analysis of how a *believing* mind is inspired through the Bible; the topic of conversion, while closely related, is beyond the limits of this study.

As was mentioned previously, the point or intention of the doctrine of creation is to affirm the relatedness of all parts of the universe to God. Or, to say the same thing, "creation" is the doctrine which affirms that "all reality is potentially and in fact the bearer of God's presence and the instrument of divine action on our behalf."[21] The Bible is surely a part of this reality and, even more, has been taken by evangelicals to be the pre-eminent human instrument of divine activity on our behalf. How, then, does the believing mind make the transition from apprehending the biblical message to apprehending that message as divine initiation with respect to salvation?

In reading any book, including the Bible, there are three "moments" or stages of mental operation.[22] The first may be called "transition." This is the moment in which the mind deliberately turns from what it was doing previously and decides to restrict itself to a single course of information: whatever is contained in the book. Implicit in this transition is the possibility of being changed as a result. That is, the mind decides to limit itself to a message or story which it will criticize or evaluate with respect to meaningfulness or significance to itself. That is what is meant by reading with an open mind. An open mind is closed only to being closed and is temporarily open only to a single source of information, always with the potential of being changed as a result of the encounter with that information. The first stage, then, is a moment of voluntary activity on the part of the mind.

"Transition" is replete with possibility, but in actuality it is replete only with critical possibility, because there are many ways that the mind would resist or reject being changed by the message of the book. Each reader has a prehistory before reading the book, and that prehistory forms a horizon of real possibilities beyond which it is extremely unlikely that the mind would be moved to change.[23]

The second moment of mental activity may be called "understanding," meaning very literally that the mind stands under the message of the book and receives it. The intention of the mind is now to receive what the author contributed or deposited in the book. This is also a critical activity, but it is unlike the critical activity of the moment of transition. Here the mind exercises a more scientific criticism in attempting to go behind the physical words on the page in order to determine what the author is saying and, more importantly, why the author is saying it. Thus, in the second stage the reader must simultaneously juggle several kinds of critical standards: the kind or genre of book, the author's expressed purpose (if any), the types of characters in the book, the methodology or organization of the book, the logical progression of the story line (or message) from beginning to end, and so on. The critical activity here is more scientific or objective than in the moment of transition simply because more people are involved. Authors write to audiences, and those audiences over time have formulated rules or standards for interpreting what they read. While neither the formulation nor the application of such rules is an exact science, it is objective in that both an author and an audience are involved; neither may afford to think that he or she is the only legitimate subject of interpretive rules. The criticism of the first moment is entirely constituted by the horizon of the concrete individual, while the criticism of the second moment, at least in principle, reflects the horizon of all humanity.

This stage, while not completely passive, is largely so. What is meant by "passive" here is that the mind responds to, or is acted upon by, data which it does not originate and over which it has little if any therapeutic control. This is seen both by the fact that the mind stands under the words and message of the author and also that it stands under the hermeneutical (interpretive) rules worked out within the literary community in history. In actually reading a book, therefore, a person is acted upon by several external sources and criteria and to that degree is a passive agent.

However, he or she is not totally passive in this moment. The mind must still consciously and deliberately activate the intention to stand under the author's words. It must also choose certain criteria over others as it encounters more and more chunks of material, so that, for example, a narrative work is not confused with and misread as a historical work.[24] On balance, though, the reader is responsible to the greatest number of objective or external sources in this moment of reading a book. This is the time when the author has greatest access to the mind and life of the reader and is likewise the time when the reader is most consciously open to the message of the author.

The third moment of mental activity in reading a book may be called "appropriation." This moment is almost entirely critical and is thus actively deliberative. It is the stage in which what the reader has encountered in the book is filtered through the grid of his or her own horizon of expectations for the purpose of determining its temporal practical effects for his or her life. In simpler language, what occurs here is the actual acceptance or rejection of various aspects of the book's perceived message. The perceived message may or may not be coincident with the author's intended message but, strictly speaking, this is irrelevant to the reader.[25] Once the reader has moved from the second moment to the third, a transition which may occur many times in the course of a single book, the reader has surrounded the author's message and made it his or her own.[26] Simultaneously, the reader evaluates that message with respect to its fit or appropriateness for his or her life.

There are two levels of evaluation which can occur within this moment. Of these, the latter is of greater interest to our theory of inspiration. At the first level of evaluation, the reader's horizon of expectations is brought to bear upon the message of the book in such a way as to determine how well it may fit within that horizon. Usually, therefore, the reader's life is modified only slightly at this level. If, for example, the reader has already accepted the eighth commandment ("You shall not steal") as his or her own, then it is unlikely that reading a newly revised set of textual copyright regulations will significantly modify his or her activity, since copyright laws are a specific application of this commandment to the publishing field. A given copyright regulation may be new to the reader, but it will still fit within his or her horizon of expectations which already proscribe theft.

At the second level of evaluation, though, the situation is reversed. Here it is more the case that the message of the book is brought to bear upon the reader's horizon of expectations. The grid itself is evaluated, and if a change of the grid or horizon is deemed appropriate, then larger and potentially major areas of the person's life will likewise be affected. Think, for instance, of a husband who has grown up accepting the surface meaning of Pauline injunctions concerning "male headship" in families. If this person then reflects upon what many have called the sexism of such injunctions for the present and changes his concept of the marriage so that it incorporates a greater parity between husband and wife, then it is clearly the case that his horizon has been restructured and that his future activity will correspondingly be altered.

It is essential to notice at both of these levels of evaluation that change is introduced not capriciously but rather with respect to a previously accepted criterion. At the first level, this criterion is straightforwardly located within the horizon of expectations. At the second level, it is still located within the horizon but at a different place from that subset of expectations which is being re-evaluated.[27] The second level of evaluation is especially interesting for a theory of inspiration because the critical priority of various subsets of that horizon is rearranged, so that what was previously less dominant *but nonetheless present* is now taken to be more dominant. In the example above, the parity of husband and wife, while probably accepted by the husband in some areas, is not taken to be the dominant model of marriage before the completion of the second level of evaluation. What is taken to be dominant is the male headship (or hierarchical) model. After the second level of evaluation, however, the hierarchical model is dominated by the parity model, even though some aspects of hierarchy may remain. The significance of noticing this with respect to inspiration is that the rearrangement of one's expectations is triggered or initiated by something external to the reader's expectations but still consonant with them. The husband has been inspired to see the former relationship in a new light.[28] Whereas the parity model was previously operative only to a minor degree, but was still present within the husband's horizon, he now sees it as the primary marital model by virtue of an illumination from within his horizon of expectations, and he changes his actions accordingly.

It was said earlier that "biblical inspiration" refers to the transition from apprehending the biblical message to apprehending it as divine initiation in salvation, that is, as God's message. But how, in the instance we have been exploring, is the transition made to the new model of marriage being a part of *God's* message to the husband? It is relatively easy to trace the bare operation of inspiration here, for much the same analysis could be applied to this case as was applied earlier to the case of teacher-student inspiration offered by Abraham. But Abraham's account failed to analyze the specific question of God's participation in the process of inspiration, and I criticized him precisely on that score. Thus, we need to address that question ourselves: how is it possible to account for the evangelical's insistence that "biblical inspiration" is in the final analysis the inspiration of persons by God?

My response to this question builds directly upon the anthropology outlined in this section and the previous one. If all of reality is God's creation, then He may use any part of it to reveal Himself to persons. If, in addition, human beings are created in God's image, then they constitutively know the truth about God even when, as rebels, they seek to repress that truth. What is essential to grasp, though, is that it is analytic to the concept of human beings that they know God. In the instance of the husband whose understanding of marriage is rearranged by reflecting upon certain biblical texts, then it is proper to say that his new understanding is inspired by God to the extent that it is consonant with what he constitutively knows about God. That is, his new understanding is more closely aligned with his knowledge of God than was his older understanding. The specific reason why we may say that this is inspiration by God is not just that he now has a better model of marriage with which to operate, but more importantly because the new model more accurately illustrates and clarifies his understanding of God for him. This is the crux of our theory of biblical inspiration. Biblical inspiration involves a person's learning more about himself or herself from reading the Bible and in the process coming to know more about God. Because knowledge of God is constitutive, however, *persons cannot learn about God except ultimately by learning from God.*[29] If the husband did not have a clearer understanding of God as a result of his new understanding of marriage gained from reflecting upon the Bible, there would be no reason to say that he had been biblically inspired. But if he has come to know God better as a result of this rearrangement, then it is both proper and unavoidable to say that God inspired it within him.

This section had two purposes. The first was to explain how the mind operates in the reading of any book, including but not limited to the Bible. I asserted that there are three moments of mental activity in this enterprise. Furthermore, I advanced the hypothesis that, while inspiration of necessity includes all three moments, it is most clearly seen in the final moment of appropriation, because this is the "time" when a person actively accepts the book's perceived message as his or her own message. My second purpose was to account for how some acts of inspiration could legitimately be called acts of divine inspiration. With respect to this question, I concluded that an act of inspiration is "divine" when a person comes to know God better as a result of a change in his or her horizon of expectations. "To know God better" assumes a prior (but less clear) knowledge of God, which is exactly what our anthropology asserts with respect to all human beings. All persons constitutively know God, and thus cannot learn about Him except ultimately by learning from Him.

Conclusion

This chapter has considered the matter of theological anthropology. It was argued that a Christian anthropology always takes human beings as dependent upon God, whether with respect to human existence in general or to thinking and moral acts in particular. Thus, in principle, all acts of knowing are acts inspired by God. Such acts are conclusions to the process of choosing, and this is the process at stake in the doctrine of humans being made in the image of God. When acts of knowing result in a greater understanding of both the world and of God, then it is proper to say that a person has been divinely inspired. The next chapter will focus on the middle term of the concept of biblical inspiration, the Bible.

4

Inspiration and the Means

Although Chapter 3 concluded with the crux of our understanding of biblical inspiration, our task is not yet complete. Thus far we have analyzed how the believing mind accepts or appropriates various data which, upon reflection, it recognizes as having come from God. In the process of this analysis we discovered that biblical inspiration is a subset or species of inspiration, and thus its meaning is enhanced to the degree that we understand how inspiration functions in general. We also discovered that biblical inspiration is a subset of divine inspiration and that the criterion of divine inspiration is whether or not a given person or community has come to know God better as a result of its newly enhanced horizon of expectations. An implication of this discussion is that, strictly speaking, all acts of inspiration are retrospectively realized. That is, one never enters a situation expecting to be inspired in a certain way. Were that the case, the expectation would logically and chronologically precede the situation and thus obviate any enhancement. One may know beforehand that an enhancement is needed, but one cannot know precisely how it will manifest itself within a given situation.[1]

This last point seems at odds, though, with what the evangelical community has characteristically confessed about the Bible. Evangelicals have long insisted that the Bible is inspired regardless of whether a given individual or community agrees that it is. They have done so especially by means of three assertions: that the Bible is verbally inspired, that it is plenarily inspired, and that it is inerrant. If the present proposal concerning biblical inspiration intends to remain within the evangelical community, therefore, we shall need to consider these three confessional doctrines, doctrines which at least initially appear to inform us about the Bible itself rather than about the reflective interaction of the believing community with it.

I shall conclude that the major value of the doctrine of verbal inspiration is to remind the church that salvation is received, not generated, by human beings. Then, after considering and challenging the traditional understanding of plenary inspiration, I will offer a reinterpretation which is better on at least three counts: it is more faithful to the church's experience with the Bible, it is more reflective of the norms of biblical scholarship, and it serves to license the pluralism or transdenominationalism of evangelicalism. Finally, I will conclude on both theological and historical grounds that the doctrine of the Bible's inerrancy should no longer be held by evangelicals. In fact, we will see that even those who profess to hold to inerrancy do not in fact hold to it. Although it might be thought that not much remains of an *evangelical* doctrine of biblical inspiration at this point, I would argue exactly the opposite: only a doctrine which is theologically tenable and which mirrors the practice of the evangelical community can claim to be evangelical.

The Verbal Inspiration of the Bible

The doctrine of verbal inspiration states that not only the message or content of Scripture, but even the very words themselves, were chosen by God to be used by the biblical author. As we have seen, the mechanics of how this choice was actualized are variously explained. The most direct explanation is the dictation theory, but the acceptance of conceptual and textual criticism by evangelicals (much less by nonevangelicals) forced the abandonment of all explicit theories of dictation. Ever since that abandonment, evangelicals have largely divided into two camps: those who reject the word but not the effect of dictation and those who seek to account for verbal inspiration in categories more closely approximating the operations of divine providence. We have seen representatives of both camps already in this study. But why did evangelicals struggle to retain the concept of verbal inspiration at all, regardless of how they explained it?

Two responses to this question will serve to account for the tenacity with which evangelicals hold to verbal inspiration. The first derives directly from the understanding of the effects of sin by the evangelical community. Because sin is seen to reflect a radical breach between God and humans, no human effort per se is able to overcome it. If, therefore, persons are to enjoy a restored bond with God, then the point of contact between God and humanity must itself result from the initiative of God. But, more concretely, if persons are to be able to be certain of salvation, then this point of contact must be constituted in such a manner as to preclude any distance between the divine intention in Scripture and the human reception of Scripture. In other words, if the intention of Scripture (human salvation) is to be apprehended with the degree of certainty requisite to overcome the radical breach of sin, then the certainty of communicating that intention from God to the human community must exceed anything which that community itself is capable of generating. The doctrine of verbal inspiration thus insists that both the meaning of Scripture and the words which bear that meaning were chosen by God precisely because of the need for salvation on the one hand and the human inability to contribute to it on the other.

The roots of this explanation of the origin of religious certainty extend to that theory of knowledge which philosophers call foundationalism and which we have already encountered in Chapter 1 under the names of naïve inductivism and Scottish realism.[2] At root, these philosophical alternatives attempt to account for the certainty of scientific knowledge which was taken by nearly all persons to constitute the difference between pre- and post-Enlightenment theories of knowledge. What accounted for the increase of certainty among the latter class of theories was precisely their empirical foundation upon those things taken as undeniable "facts." Certainty was thus ultimately embedded in fact, in what could not be denied without dispensing with certainty altogether. Or, to say the same thing, the certainty of knowledge was taken to be embedded in the psychological need for knowledge to be certain in order for it to count as knowledge. Whatever was taken as objective "fact," therefore, was precisely correlative to whatever it was that accounted for the human need for knowledge to be certain.

For evangelicals, there was little question of what among all of the various alternatives could stand as "fact": the Bible. More precisely, it was what actually constituted the Bible, the words which comprised it as a book. There was nothing more fundamental than the words of the Bible in which the certainty requisite for human salvation could be located—not their present meaning, the author's intentions, their meaning as understood by the original believing audience, or their meaning as determined by lexical usage in the primitive world. The validity of each of these alternatives was taken to rest upon the biblical word, and thus only that word was sufficient as the locus or holder of religious certainty.

The second reason why evangelicals insist that inspiration is verbal is closely related to the first. It is consistently referred to by evangelicals as the fear of subjectivism. Stated simply, subjectivism is the presumption of the autonomy of the human subject, and thus is a precise denial of the anthropology summarized above. Evangelicals resisted subjectivism in principle because the autonomous human subject is a completely inadequate locus of certainty regarding God and human salvation. What we called the evangelical anthropology asserts that persons are entirely the object of the divine initiative. With respect to matters divine, human beings learn about God by learning from Him. The alternative possibility, that persons could initiate matters with respect both to salvation and to the certainty of the knowledge of salvation, was taken by evangelicals not just as wrong but as constituting the grossest sort of rebelliousness against God.

What may we learn from the insistence upon biblical inspiration as a property of the words of the Bible per se? Primarily, it seems, we must appreciate the point that inspiration is not self-generated. This is an analytic truth, of course, and thus it is seemingly obvious.[3] As I have often noted, the concept of inspiration requires at least two mentally active agents and a medium. Apart from this structure, and apart from the initiating activity of one agent by means of the medium and the receiving activity of the other by means of the same medium, there can be no concept of inspiration.[4]

The evangelicals were not just making a conceptual point, however. In the larger context from which most evangelical theories of inspiration sprang, a context which looked with great suspicion upon any alleged act of God in the world and upon any theory of moral anthropology which retained vestiges of the debilitating effects of sin, evangelical theories of biblical inspiration struggled to retain the traditional Christian structure of the God-human relationship. The redefinition of this bond within post-Enlightenment Protestantism was taken by evangelicals to be a fatal redefinition because in their eyes it reversed the roles of the initiating and receiving agents. But, since the "new" initiating agent was precisely the person who stood in need of what he or she was now said to initiate, human salvation became impossible. The Bible became more a commentary on salvation than the primary means of it.

In insisting upon the traditional structure of the God-human relationship according to which God, not persons, prompts the activity of salvation, evangelicals reminded the Christian community that knowledge *of* God must ultimately be seen as knowledge *from* God if it is to be a saving knowledge. That is, knowledge of the divine originates outside humans. This is the most significant conclusion, I believe, to be drawn from discussions concerning the verbal inspiration of the Bible.

Unfortunately, discussions of verbal inspiration have generally tended to confuse this point in the very attempt to make it. By making the locus of certainty the biblical word itself rather than the actual experience of salvation by means of that word, evangelicals committed two errors. The first is that they took certainty as a property of words rather than as a property of the mind. But that is not how certainty operates. The mind accepts a given set of words as certain when it sees a correspondence between them and concrete actuality. Logically, experience always precedes the reflection upon experience by words. Were the situation otherwise, there could be no criteria by which to distinguish between true and false statements and observations.

In referring to certainty as a property of the biblical words, it is clear that the evangelicals' goal was to affirm the normative status of the Bible over other categories of religious data. I agree with this goal, but I cannot agree with the tactic which confuses the object to which certainty attaches. Certainty is the conclusion of a judgment, and judgments are acts of human minds rather than properties of objects such as words. Said differently, certainty results from mental judgments, and such judgments are themselves the results of comparisons which the mind makes over several primary data of experience. A *certain* judgment is one which chooses a given explanation or theory as correct as over against others in accounting for concrete actuality as the person or community experiences it. With respect to the Bible, therefore, certainty results from the mental determination which chooses the biblical accounts of redemption and salvation as those which best summarize the actual experience of salvation undergone by Christian believers. As such, it properly calls attention to the mediatorial or sacramental status of the Bible because it refers to that act of the mind which grasps the Biblical accounts of salvation as those which best convey the intention of God toward the believing community and ultimately toward the entire world.

The second confusion which characteristically arises from evangelical discussions concerning verbal inspiration is that they are dictation theories in all but name. In spite of the vehemence with which this point is denied, it is impossible to construct a theory of the unique and divine status of a given set of words (i. e., those comprising the Bible) without simultaneously constructing a theory of dictation. Once it is assumed that human moral fallibility is unable to be utilized by God as a vehicle of divine inspiration, and it is instead assumed that the doctrines of biblical certainty and perspicuity require the overriding of fallible contributions to Scripture, then some form of dictation is present. I am not alone in noticing this, of course, and do not wish to belabor the point. For the moment, I shall simply note that evangelicals failed to take seriously the mediatorial status of the Bible and instead operated as though it were the divine terminus of the divine-human encounter. I shall further inspect this misconception in the section dealing with inerrancy below.

We have now accomplished our first real interpretive work. We accepted a formal element within characteristically evangelical theories of biblical inspiration but suggested a somewhat different material significance for it. I suggested that the point of talk of the verbal inspiration of the Bible is to remind the believing audience that humans always respond to God and do so especially in the matter of the divine salvation to which the Bible witnesses. Salvation is not self-generated and thus its inspiration within persons is not either. We denied, however, that the doctrine of verbal inspiration has anything to do with empirical properties which the biblical words, unlike all other words in the world, possess per se. Were that the case, then one would have to accept the divine status of those words before understanding them; one would have to be saved in order to become saved. Our theory of inspiration intends to be more faithful to the nature of experience by emphasizing that experience always precedes reflection. In particular, this means that those who refer to the Bible as verbally inspired have already experienced divine salvation in ways which are consonant with the ways summarized and presented in it.

The Plenary Inspiration of the Bible

We now turn to the second of the three characteristically evangelical confessions about the Bible, that concerning its "plenary" or full inspiration. Traditionally, the doctrine of plenary inspiration has been understood in two ways. The first is that all parts of the Bible are equally inspired. More concretely, the divine authority which is taken as consequent to inspiration is equally available in all parts of the Bible. Thus, regardless of where one turns in the Bible, the doctrine of plenary inspiration affirms that one will encounter the word of God there rather than the word of human beings only. This is its inclusive meaning.

The second or exclusive significance of plenary inspiration is that only the Bible is assured of being the written word of God. This is not to deny the possibility of the written word existing outside of the Bible, since in principle at least a book or letter may yet be discovered which deserves to be in the canon. But, with respect to present-day actualities, plenary inspiration asserts that the Bible is sufficient for salvation and that any extrabiblical material which intends to contribute to salvation does so only to the degree that it corresponds to Scripture.

The present section will provide a brief critique of the traditional conception of plenary inspiration. On the basis of that critique, I shall then suggest an interpretation which not only avoids the weakness of the traditional understanding but additionally serves to license the third of the three distinctives of evangelicalism, that is, its transdenominational character.

The primary problem with the traditional understanding of the doctrine of plenary inspiration is that it does not accurately reflect the actual experience of the Christian church.[5] That is, while the doctrine of plenary inspiration asserts that all portions of the Bible are equally authoritative because they are equally inspired of God, the actual experience of the church indicates just the opposite. Certain books and texts have characteristically surfaced as being of greater significance to the church, while others have never emerged as concretely authoritative. The ecclesial area in which this assertion is most easily verified is liturgy, and in particular preaching. It is not my intent here statistically to quantify this assertion, aside from recalling the reader's own experiences as a participant in a worshipping congregation. Instead, I shall ask why it is that certain texts have, and have not, proven formative in the life of the Christian church. Why, that is, do some biblical texts become authoritative in fact while others remain only nominally normative? And what implications does this question have for those who see a continuing usefulness for the notion of plenary inspiration?[6]

For most of the church's history, the diversity of culture has not had much theological significance. By "the diversity of culture" I mean the different outlooks upon the world generated by, or at least concomitant with, different groupings of peoples. Bernard Lonergan refers to that which distinguishes among groups of persons as "differentiated consciousness" and has categorized various forms of differentiated consciousness around five types.[7] "The diversity of culture" thus refers to the pluralism of meanings of experience generated by the collision of persons or groups who have different types of outlooks. The diversity of culture as a *theological* problem is how the truth of the gospel, God's self-revelation which presumably does not vary with time, is communicated to historical peoples whose understanding does vary with respect to time and their own particular outlooks.[8]

Armed with this understanding of the human world as divided into groupings distinguished by characteristic outlooks upon human experience, we may now address this theological problem, or what may be called the unevenness of biblical normativity. Why, that is, do certain texts function authoritatively in the church's life while others do not? It is precisely this unevenness which the traditional understanding of plenary inspiration obscures, concentrating as it does upon biblical inspiration as a simple category of a book rather than as a complex category of at least two agents and a medium. If, however, this latter scheme is a more accurate reflection of the phenomenon of inspiration, and if there is no simple comprehensive way to characterize the receiving agents of inspiration, as Lonergan's analysis indicates, then we may say that the unevenness of biblical normativity arises precisely from the pluralism of ways in which the world is experienced by persons. This of necessity implies a pluralism of theologies of (or ways of thinking about) salvation, since Christian salvation is always salvation *in* the world in which we as concrete humans live. Certain types of human consciousness or outlooks will naturally respond to certain biblical ways of characterizing salvation, while other types will respond better to other biblical ways. In principle, no one way of correlating one's experience of salvation with a biblical characterization of salvation is superior to another way of correlating them since one cannot learn about God except by learning from God. In practice, of course, certain ways of making this correlation will be found to be more expressive for some groupings of persons within the church than for others. If I am correct in this analysis, then the doctrine of the plenary inspiration of the Bible should be taken to refer to the range of outlooks within the human community, each of which is able to articulate its own experience of salvation with direct reference to stories and images contained within the Bible.

An example from the New Testament will serve to illustrate this latter assertion. It has only been within the relatively recent past that biblical scholars have recognized that the titles used for Jesus in the New Testament were confessional or credal in nature rather than ontological. That is, titles such as "Messiah" "Son of Man," "Lord," and so on[9] are indications of the significance of the faith which the communities that used them had in Jesus rather than abstract descriptions of who Jesus was in himself or per se. Thus, we would expect to find the title "Messiah" used by Jewish Christians because the term already had a religious meaning within Judaism which it did not have, for example, for converts in Greece and Italy. As James Dunn notes in his discussion of the title, however, Jesus himself seems to have resisted the usefulness of "Messiah" precisely because of the nationalist and political connotations it had while he was alive.[10] Clearly, then, "Messiah" (and its Greek translation "Christ") acquired specific Christian significance from its usefulness to the Jewish Christian community rather than from its usage by Jesus. This community advanced or enriched the meaning of "Messiah" so that it came to refer to the humble person whose suffering and death signaled divine vindication, over the earlier narrower meaning according to which suffering and death were taken as indications of God's disapproval and rejection (which is the meaning that Jesus rejected). The Jewish Christians accomplished this development by linking together what had previously been unconnected: contribution to the Kingdom of God by the glorious messiah on the one hand and the suffering, humiliation, and death of the suffering servant of Isaiah 53 on the other. Because Jesus was the focus of their worship and thus stood fully vindicated before God in their eyes, they felt licensed in developing the notion of messiahship to include what was foolishness to non-Christian Jews: a crucified messiah.[11]

On the other hand, a large number of early Christians existed for whom the phrase "Jesus is the Messiah" did not serve as the primary confession. This appears to be true of, among others, Hellenistic Jewish Christians, that is, Palestinian Jews whose predominant culture was Greek rather than Hebrew and who became Christian converts as adults. For this community, "Messiah" had to be supplemented in order to express what was for them the highest possible religious affirmation; by itself "Messiah" did not adequately summarize their faith in the risen Jesus as it had for the former community. The most common supplement given to "Messiah" within this community was "Son of God." There is evidence of this supplementation in Peter's great confession in Matthew 16:16, where Matthew explains Mark's terse

"You are the Christ" (Mark 8:29) by adding the phrase " . . . the Son of the living God." John reflects the same need to explain "Messiah" when he announces the reason for writing his Gospel (John 20:31): " . . . these things are written so that you may believe that Jesus is the Christ, the Son of God. . . . " While these two examples do not at all exhaust the total number available in the New Testament, they do serve to indicate how confessional statements were tailored to reflect the existing religious character of the community whose faith they were intended to express. Hellenistic Jewish Christians could scarcely be expected to represent their faith adequately by means of credal statements which were not natively their own.

This example is helpful, I believe, because it illustrates how different cultures utilized different confessions to summarize their common faith in the risen Jesus. In addition, however, and perhaps just as important for the purposes of this study, it illustrates the actual practice of biblical inspiration at work among a variety of Christian groups in the first century. Both "Messiah" and "Son of God" are Old Testament images. That is, both were biblical images to the Jew of the first century. Both "Hebrew" and "Hellenistic" Jews felt the need to refer to their experience of salvation in Jesus by means of images which were relevantly distinct from each other but were nonetheless commonly drawn from their Bible. In the one case, "Messiah" provided a sufficient category by which to affirm the divine significance of Jesus, provided that the concept be consonant with (i.e., inspired by) the image of the suffering servant of Isaiah 53 rather than the image of the conquering political hero. In the other case, "Messiah" was only tangentially helpful and had to be supplemented by the image of "Son of God" drawn from Psalms 2:7 ("He said to me, 'You are my son, today I have begotten you.'") and from 2 Samuel 7:14 ("I will be his father, and he will be my son."), both of which corresponded to Jesus's use of *abba* in reference to God. In both instances, we see at work in the Bible what this study takes as being present within all specific acts of biblical inspiration: a community's understanding of God enhanced by the creative interaction of an existing authoritative document with the present needs of a given people. And in both instances we see this creative interaction occurring only after the experience of salvation by Jesus; it is only in the light of *that* reality that either type of Jewish Christian looked to the Bible as source of images by which to summarize their faith and to communicate it to others.

If we understand plenary inspiration in the ways just presented, that is, as a reflection on the process by which a variety of Christian groups validates the Christianness of their experiences of salvation by means of images drawn from the Bible which are meaningful to their particular group, then we have at the same time provided a theological warrant for evangelicalism's pluralistic or transdenominational character. I do not intend to commend the genesis of every denomination and movement within Christendom, of course. But I do intend to call attention to the formal similarity which exists between pluralistic contemporary evangelicalism on the one hand and pluralistic primitive Christianity on the other. Evangelicalism affirms the actual priority of the experience of salvation over the reflection upon it by means of certain doctrinal statements and accepts the affirmation of the reality of that experience as the only prerequisite for theological unity. Structural considerations (such as episcopal, presbyterial, or charismatic hierarchies) and other theological considerations (such as infant or believer's baptism) are all subordinate to the issue of whether a community and its members have experienced God's forgiving mercy in Jesus and whether they refer to that salvation by images which are either drawn from or consonant with the Bible. This is not to say that those other issues are not important but only that they are secondary to that which distinguishes Christianity from all other religions: the experience of God's salvation in Jesus of Nazareth.

In summary, I believe that the plenary inspiration of the Bible is most intelligible when it, like all other aspects of the doctrine of inspiration, is interpreted primarily from the perspective of the recipient of inspiration. Human beings differ widely both in their experiences and in their reflections upon their experiences. No characterization of persons can be successful if it overlooks or flattens out these differences. The understanding of plenary inspiration offered here recognizes such differences among human beings. It likewise affirms that the various characterizations of Christian salvation which exist in the Bible are themselves the reflections of how differing groups of early Christians wrote about their shared, but not identical, experiences of God in Jesus. Each such characterization thus constitutes a model or paradigm for how the experience of salvation may be cast into conceptual terms in the present. Plenary inspiration denies that any single characterization may be viewed as sufficient. On the contrary, it insists that the entire range of models forms the means through which God is able to bring about relatively regulated, and hence canonical, reflections upon salvation. It is in the conjunction of the initial experience of salvation with the biblical patterns of thinking about it that contemporary Christians share in the faith of the church of all ages.

The Inerrancy of the Bible

"Biblical inerrancy" has become such a part of the identity of American fundamentalism and of some strands of evangelicalism that most American Christians do not know what either stands for apart from it. To be fair, this constriction of the significance of evangelicalism to one particular doctrine within it results as much from those who stand within this branch of the church as from those outside of it.[12] The task of this chapter is not to retrace the route of this process of constriction. Rather, it is to consider whether the notion of inerrancy has any continuing usefulness to the doctrine of biblical inspiration, especially that understanding of inspiration being developed in this study. I shall discuss briefly the meaning of inerrancy and the primary reason why I believe it has occupied such a prominent position in Christian reflections upon the significance of the Bible. I shall then turn to Donatism, an intense controversy in the early church whose "orthodox" resolution will help in determining whether or not the notion of error has any theological relevance to the saving operation of God in the world. I shall conclude that it does not and therefore that the notion of the inerrancy of the Bible should be dropped as a constituent of the doctrine of biblical inspiration.

The idea or notion of inerrancy is very simple. Harold Lindsell describes it for us:

> Inspiration may be defined as the inward work of the Holy Spirit in the hearts and minds of chosen men who then wrote the Scriptures so that God got written what He wanted. The Bible in all of its parts constitutes the written Word of God to man. This Word is free from all error in its original autographs. . . . It is wholly trustworthy in matters of history and doctrine. . . . [The] authors of Scripture, under the guidance of the Holy Spirit, were preserved from making factual, historical, scientific, or other errors. The Bible does not purport to be a textbook of history, science, or mathematics; yet when the writers of Scripture spoke of matters embraced in these disciplines, they did not indite error; they wrote what was true. . . . Inspiration involved infallibility [13] from start to finish. God the Holy Spirit by nature cannot lie or be the author of untruth. If the Scripture is inspired at all, it must be infallible. If any part of it is not infallible, then that part cannot be inspired. If inspiration allows for the possibility of error then inspiration ceases to be inspiration. [14]

A summary would be that the Bible is free from all errors because it is God's Word and God cannot lie. There are three conceptual difficulties rooted in this position. Taken together with Donatism, these objections render inerrancy obsolete as a topic of interest to the inspiration of the Bible.

The first difficulty with the traditional inerrancy position is that it is not at all consonant with the concept of inspiration. I have argued repeatedly here that any act of inspiration involves at least two mentally active agents and a medium, or means, through which the receiving agent is indirectly changed by the initiating agent. As Lindsell makes clear, however, the inerrancy position rearranges these factors so that only the biblical author receives inspiration, which then results in the writing of books. Thus, the operation of inspiration occurs exclusively to the biblical author, but never since then. That is, only the biblical authors were religiously inspired in the sense of coming to understand more about God, and this not from reflection upon their concrete experiences of salvation but rather from a direct and unmediated communication of God to them. The basis on which all other believers grow in faith is not only noninspirational but is nonreligious as well: the inerrancy of the records left by those authors. This, then, entails an impossible choice, namely, that inerrancy per se is a religious phenomenon, which it clearly is not, or that believers mature in their faith by means of phenomena ("true" documents) which have no obvious relation to the experiences of salvation. In making the Bible itself the terminus of divine inspiration rather than the means of it, the inerrancy position makes the maturing of faith dependent on a purely intellectual concept: the evaluation of truth claims. For the conscientious inerrantist, therefore, growth in salvation must always be postponed until all of the relevant factors in the truth claim may be adjudicated. As even the brief history of historical criticism has demonstrated, this process is interminable. Worse yet, it occurs entirely outside of the believer; in systematic terms, it calls only for *notitia* rather than *fiducia*.

The second general difficulty with the inerrancy position outlined by Lindsell is that it identifies the Bible with God, or the sign with the thing signified.[15] This difficulty has already been discussed in Chapter 1. Theologically it may be said to originate in a confusion between different meanings of the phrase "the Word of God." Christian theologians have traditionally distinguished between the written and the incarnate Word of God. The former meaning refers to the message of the Bible and in particular to the good news of salvation.

Here it is important to recall the referential status of language. Language is comprised of individual words and various groupings of them which refer to objects or entities beyond themselves. Because words are human and cultural creations, these objects or entities may be referred to by several different groupings of words. There are several ways to refer to the same conceptual object (message or meaning), just as there are several ways to refer to the same physical object. (A "successful" reference is ultimately determined by the audience, as was discussed in the previous section.) The message or meaning of the written word of God (human salvation) is one, but the words used to refer to it are many and varied. Such is not the case with the incarnate word of God, however. Here there is an identity of the sign and the reality, that is, of the human person and the divine activity on behalf of the world. Apart from Jesus there would be no incarnation of the saving message of God. For Christians, therefore, compatibility with the biblical understanding of the Jesus event constitutes the criterion by which all words used about God are evaluated as more or less appropriate, including the statements of the gospel message in the Bible itself.[16] So, while both the gospel and Jesus are called the Word of God, they are not equally the Word of God; the incarnation determines or controls the meaning of the gospel in a way that the gospel does not determine or control it.

The significance of this ambiguity for our present purposes is that inerrancy discussions ascribe to the words of the Bible an attribute which only God may be said to possess: intrinsic freedom from error. In so doing they not only falsify the nature of language, but they also relativize the significance of Jesus for Christian theology. For inerrantists, but not for those who wrote the New Testament, the Christianness of one's experience of salvation is controlled by fidelity to Jesus *and* by logical compatibility with all of the various ways of confessing faith in Jesus within the New Testament. The New Testament thus becomes a Procrustean bed rather than a pattern or model for the controlled ("canonical") growth of confessions of the significance of Jesus appropriate to various believing communities. Inerrantist inspiration has nothing to do with the enhancement of one's self-understanding and understanding of God. Instead, it refers to the production of a static set of words with no reference at all to modern believers as recipients and interpreters of God's self-revelation. As seen in this study, however, such an understanding accords neither with the definition of inspiration nor with its operation as seen in various communities of first-century believers. [17]

The third difficulty we shall deal with has to do with the significance of purported errors in the Bible with respect to the existence of faith within a Christian community. The method of this study insists that the experience of salvation (or "faith") always chronologically precedes theology, for theology is the discipline of understanding faith. The inerrancy position, however, states that faith, or the prior experience of God as savior, is impossible if errors exist in the Bible, since the believer could never be certain of the truth of God's self-revelation if such errors existed there.

Inerrantists have long maintained that it is only the autographs, those papyri, skins, or clay tablets that were physically inscribed by the biblical authors, which are inerrant. Room is thus allowed for the existence of "difficulties" (i.e., errors) which all have encountered in contemporary translations of the Bible without actually diminishing the meaningfulness of the inerrancy argument itself. The significance of this concession on the part of inerrantists does not lie in the area where it has most often been exploited, namely, the artificiality of the argument based on the irretrievability of the autographs. [18] Instead, it lies in noticing that the inerrantists themselves allow for errors in the very Bibles which they use authoritatively in their churches. The claim that both the authority of Scripture and the certainty of salvation would be nullified if there were errors in the Bible is belied by the practice of those persons who make that claim and yet continue to use their modern and errant copies of the Bible authoritatively. If admittedly errant Bibles are religiously useful and authoritative for inerrantists, why perpetuate the abstract argument for the inerrancy of irretrievable autographs? The only reason would seem to be to safeguard the doctrine of the truthfulness of God, an instinct which is proper but which concerns the doctrine of God rather than the doctrine of Scripture and thus, strictly speaking, is off the subject. If the purpose of theology is to reflect upon the actual experience of believers, then that reflection must consider all that the believer experiences.[19]

The final topic to consider in our assessment of inerrancy is the Donatist schism of the fourth- and fifth-century African church. Although Donatism was primarily an ecclesiastical controversy, we shall explore it to mine its lessons for the present controversy concerning the "purity" of the Bible.

By the beginning of the fourth century, the Catholic faith had taken firm hold in most of North Africa. Before Constantine, though, who became Roman emperor in 306 and legalized Christianity in 313, sporadic persecutions continued to plague African Christians. In particular, they were still reeling from "the last, the Great, Persecution of Diocletian, in 303–305."[20] Like all religious persecutions, this one brought to the surface the question of the relationship between church and culture because of the need to deal with those believers who had capitulated to and complied with the persecutors in order to avoid imprisonment and death.

This question was especially acute with respect to bishops who had surrendered copies of Scripture to the Romans. The actual proximate cause of the Donatist schism involved Bishop Mensurius of Carthage, who had handed over heretical documents to the unsuspecting Romans under the pretense that those documents were Scripture. For this act, he was accused of *traditio*. Although Mensurius died before any official action could be taken in his case, the horns of the Donatist dilemma were set. On the one hand were the "rigorists," who argued that *traditores* had forfeited all rights to ecclesiastical leadership, especially the right of ordaining priests and bishops. On the other hand were the "liberals," who maintained that proper penance absolved sinners from all errors of action and thus that *traditio* did not preclude the possibility of subsequent leadership in the church.[21] The rigorist party at Carthage quickly deposed Mensurius's successor and ordained first Majorinus and then Donatus, for whom the schism is named, in his place. The Donatists practiced widespread rebaptism and reordination since they held all Catholics to be outside the true church. Augustine, priest at Carthage and later bishop of Hippo, undertook the defense of the Catholic position.

Theologically, the Donatists separated from the Catholic faith over the question of whether a person could properly mediate divine forgiveness if he or she had committed an offense which was publicly known.[22] In response to this, Augustine first drew attention to the unwarranted restriction by the Donatists of "impurity of life" to the offense of *traditio*. That is, in insisting that the sin of *traditio* disqualified a person both from administering the sacraments and from ordaining priests and bishops, the Donatists ignored even more heinous offenses committed by their own defenders against the Catholics, including theft, arson, suicide, and murder.[23] Thus, their schismatic tendencies were demonstrated by seizing upon one legitimate doctrine within Christian thought and practice to the exclusion of others, especially the principle of ethical consistency (Matthew 7:12).

More obviously still, Donatist sectarianism is discerned in the corollary of the doctrine of purity, namely, that genuine Christian faith was to be found only in those persons who had successfully resisted handing over the seditious material to the emperor's soldiers. What this implied in turn was that the true church was objectively sinless and restricted to North Africa, since only there was apostolic authority untainted by *traditio*.[24] Augustine rejected this corollary too, stating that the true church is found wherever the sacraments are properly received and not, as the Donatists averred, only where they are properly administered.[25] It is this line of defense which is of most interest to a consideration of inerrancy.

The Donatists claimed that *traditio* placed one outside the true church, from where it was impossible properly to administer the sacraments. The theological warrant for this position was that priestly holiness or sanctity was essential to the communication of the intention of the sacrament (forgiveness and salvation) from God to the human recipient. In more contemporary language, they believed that there were three moments or aspects to a proper sacramental act: the divine intention, the public sanctity of the human mediator, and the willingness of the recipient. The Donatists claimed Cyprian as their authority. In the previous century and also in a period following persecution, he had insisted that bishops and priests be members of the true church in order for their official acts to be effective.[26] Willis points out, though, that the Donatists actually altered Cyprian's dictum in ignoring his assumption that "a bishop was not really conceivable apart from his church and people."[27] For Cyprian, as for most of the primitive church, priestly and episcopal authority was not inherent but was rather delegated by the congregation, the ultimate human seat of religious authority.[28] The Donatists (again) restricted the meaning of priestly and episcopal membership in the true church so that it referred solely to the public character of the sacramental minister. In so doing, they gratuitously elevated the second of the three aspects of a sacramental act and made the third aspect entirely dependent upon it. In other words, the reception of the divine offer of salvation was entirely relative to the personal holiness of the priest; his character was essential, rather than instrumental or mediatorial, to the efficacy of the sacrament.

In attempting theologically to overcome the schism introduced by the Donatists, Augustine faced the delicate task of at once affirming their sectarianism and welcoming them back into the Catholic church without rebaptizing their laity and reordaining their clergy, a move which would have underscored the legitimacy of the original division.

The *via media* he took was to distinguish between a sacrament itself and the use or validity of it, and thus between the *communio sacramentorum* and the *communio sanctorum*. Sacraments may be administered anywhere, he said, including outside a true church where are located both heretics and pagans (i.e., those who hold to false Christian beliefs and those who hold to no Christian beliefs). In the case of the administration of the sacraments to such persons, it is clear that the personal holiness of the minister has no relevance at all to the invalidity of such sacramental acts; it is the recipient whose presumed self-sufficiency precludes the reception of God's forgiveness and salvation. By the same token, then, the validity or benefit of a sacramental act also has to do with the openness of the recipient to God's forgiveness and to living a life of charity or tangible gratitude to God. In this way, the Donatists were seen to be schismatics, but since it was their intention in receiving baptism, communion, and ordination to be faithful to the triune God proclaimed by all of their sacramental liturgies, nothing further was required for their (re)admission to the Catholic church than the expressed intention to live charitably in the one, holy, and apostolic church.

The significance of Augustine's solution for the present controversy is clear. Formally, there is a similarity in that both inerrantists and Donatists restrict themselves to a single element within the entire corpus of Christian doctrines to evaluate the appropriateness of the beliefs of others. As we have seen, such an evaluation does not square with the practice of the first-century Christian communities, whose ultimate criterion for evaluating Christianness was experiential rather than intellectual.

More importantly, however, the Donatist controversy stands as a witness against allowing any mediating element to overwhelm and thus block the divine intention of human salvation, whether that element be bishop or book. No mediating element need possess empirically divine characteristics in order to be constituted as a mediating element, as is clear from the preceding consideration of the doctrine of God as creator. More to the point for our purposes, no reflection upon Christian experience can fail to notice that it is present copies of the Bible, which all parties admit to contain errors and difficulties, which constitute the Scripture that inspires and guides the church and its members today. Theology is a reflection upon existing faith, including but not limited to one's own, and it is therefore incoherent to hold that faith is impossible where errant mediators exist. Paradoxically, it is the presence of faith in those who insist most strongly upon inerrancy that is the greatest testimony against inerrancy.

In this section I have argued that the major warrant for the inerrancy position depends on a confusion between the doctrine of God and the doctrine of Scripture. The failure to distinguish carefully between them led historically to the attribution to the latter of a characteristic (intrinsic errorlessness) that properly belongs only to God. Furthermore, this confusion tended to give the written mediator of the God-human relationship priority over that relationship itself, which is, to say the least, contrary to sound theology. Finally, a historical analogy was discovered in Donatism which warns us against seeking perfection of any earthly instrument which God may use to enhance our knowledge and love of Him. The doctrine of God as creator means that everything God uses as means to inspire salvation is *not* God, and thus cannot be invested with characteristics which only God properly possesses.[29]

Conclusion

In this chapter I have presented an outline of a theory of biblical inspiration which I believe is faithful to the evangelical tradition and yet is, at times, a deliberate development of that tradition. If there is a single way to characterize this theory, it is that the phrase "biblical inspiration" refers to the enhancement of one's understanding of God brought about instrumentally through the Bible, rather than to the mysterious and nonrepeatable process by which "God got written what He wanted" in the Bible. In other words, "the inspiration of the Bible" refers to the enhancement which the Bible instrumentally causes in persons and not to the Bible itself as the terminus or locus of that enhancement. In grammatical terms, my theory views "the inspiration of the Bible" as a subjective genitive rather than as an objective genitive. This means that the uniqueness of the Bible for Christian life and theology is rooted not in its inspiration, but rather in that to which it inspires us, namely, a greater understanding and awareness of, and fidelity to, the threefold God to whom the Bible bears witness. This realization in turn invites the Christian community to reflect more fully upon any and all experiences of inspiration as analogies by which it may better understand the inspiration which the Bible mediates. I have already touched upon this task in the section concerning the activity of the mind.

The final chapter of this book deals with God, the initiator of salvation. Here we shall explore the question of how the human mind receives inspiration from God and how it may be certain that that inspiration is from God. The discussion of this matter will conclude our consideration of the three aspects of biblical inspiration which William Abraham brought to our attention.

5

God as the Initiator
of Inspiration

Thus far we have addressed ourselves to two of the three elements involved in the concept of biblical inspiration. We have seen that inspiration is a mediated enhancement of one's mind (or, more generally, one's life) which is not self-generated. Biblical inspiration, then, is inspiration which results in an enhanced understanding of God that conforms to what is said of God in the Bible. Because one cannot learn about God except by learning from Him, we may also conclude that biblical inspiration is initiated by God.

Chapter 4 discussed three topics which characterize what evangelicals have traditionally believed about the Bible as the means of inspiration. The topics were reworked so that they would be more understandable yet still conform to the characteristic norms of evangelicalism, especially the so-called formal and material principles of Protestantism. On those bases certain interpretations of verbal and plenary inspiration were proposed, and in addition we saw good reason to drop the doctrine of biblical inerrancy altogether.

In this chapter we turn to the final element in the concept of biblical inspiration: God, the initiating agent. Here I shall try to do two things. I shall first outline a theology proper (that is, a doctrine of God) which I propose as an adequate ground of our understanding of divine inspiration. Here I shall be helped especially by Karl Rahner, a Catholic theologian who has contributed much to an understanding of the ways in which God and human beings are related. I shall take from Rahner only that which contributes directly to the concept of God in order to see how God is present in the "enhancing toward salvation" of biblical inspiration. Next, I will suggest four criteria for relating divine inspiration and biblical inspiration. These criteria will constitute my final proposal for identifying biblical inspiration within the evangelical community.

The Transcendental Theology of Karl Rahner

I am not interested here in developing a detailed, critical explanation of Karl Rahner's theology.[1] Instead, I shall provide an interpretation of him by reflecting on the human phenomenon of asking and answering questions. Understanding this characteristic activity will aid us in seeing how it may be said that God is present in acts of human knowing.

I have repeatedly criticized the appropriateness of deductivist or a priori approaches in this study. Instead, I have commended that method of inquiry which pays close attention to actual human experience as the beginning point for inquiry. Thus, "the experiencing subject" is the primary, although not sufficient, criterion for evaluating anthropological analyses. The word "experiencing" is significant here, for it calls attention to the fact that the subject is not simply an isolated, private, or independent bit of the universe. It is this latter understanding of experience, and thus of "the subject," which has historically led evangelicals to be suspicious of subjectivism,[2] a suspicion which has often been well-founded. Rahner, however, calls his approach to the doctrine of God a "transcendental subjectivism," signaling by this designation that there is a way to define subjectivism other than the way which has typically been rejected by evangelicals. I will discuss transcendental subjectivism in the two stages implicit in its title.

Close attention to the phenomenon of experience helps us to see why subjectivism need not in principle be susceptible to the criticism just mentioned. Usually, experience has been assumed to be an entirely private or interior phenomenon, following from Friedrich Schleiermacher's definition of Christianity as "a feeling of absolute dependence." Since feeling is interior by definition, the phenomenon of subjective experience has likewise been taken to be interior in its entirety. However, while I do not wish to deny that interior feelings are elements of experience, they are not the exclusive constituents of it that Schleiermacher took them to be. More usually, I would argue, experience is the experience of something in the external world and thus includes an objective or external referent as well as an interior one.[3] In this more usual understanding, then, the subject is defined as "one who experiences," with experience accordingly understood as including both interior and exterior poles. Seen in this light, subjectivism is not susceptible to the charge referred to above. It is only those subjectivist methodologies that ignore the external component of human experience and knowledge which are criticized as being solipsist or privatist, and they are properly criticized because they ignore an unavoidable constituent of nearly all acts of experiencing and knowing.

Rahner qualifies his subjectivist methodology by calling it *transcendental* subjectivism. If "subjectivism" reflects Rahner's insistence that we begin our anthropological analysis with concrete human experiences, "transcendental" reflects his belief that such experiences will ultimately reveal how God and humans interact in all acts of knowing. Rahner's transcendentalism seeks to account for how God is said to ground all acts of human knowing, and therefore inspire them, without thereby asserting either that persons cease to be persons or that God communicates directly and immediately with the human mind. To say the same thing from the human perspective, Rahner's transcendentalism seeks to account for how the human intellect surpasses or transcends itself as it grows in knowledge and understanding without thereby ceasing to be itself, and how it accomplishes all of this in relation to God.

Humans are characteristically questioning beings. If this is true as a general observation, then what must be true of human beings as such in order that we express ourselves as humans by means of questioning? What does this observation allow us to discover about human beings and God? The response to this particular matter will be discovered a posteriori by reflecting upon human experience, but will exist a priori as the condition which accounts for the universality of questioning among humans.

Reflection upon the human phenomenon of asking questions leads to two conclusions. The first is that the act of questioning in itself affirms the self-recognized limitations of the questioner. That is, a subject who asks a question affirms his or her own finitude, since questioning presumes a recognized need to go beyond the present. No one questions what is fully understood and accepted, but only that which is not fully understood or fully satisfactory. Thus, the condition which accounts for the act of asking questions is perceived or recognized finitude on the part of the questioner; in the absence of such finitude, no question would ever by asked.

The second conclusion is that human beings, as characteristic questioners, are unrestrictedly open to the universe. At the moment of asking, questioners affirm their finitude, not mastery, with respect to understanding. After asking a question but before having it answered, therefore, they are open to receiving an answer from anywhere. Were this not the case, then the question itself would not be a genuine expression of finitude.[4] A question, then, represents both a recognition of dissatisfaction with respect to one's own present understanding and an openness to the universe as the storehouse of possible answers to that question.

The observation that human beings are characteristic questioners means that answered questions do not overcome the condition of finitude. That is, answers to questions simply provide an enlarged base from which to ask further questions. This is implicit in the observation that questioning is unending. Thus, the observation that humans characteristically ask questions is but another way of saying that humans are unrestrictedly finite, since the asking of questions affirms the notion of finitude, while the unceasing asking of questions affirms the notion of unceasing finitude.

It may now be said that openness to the "ever-receding horizon" of possibilities which is the storehouse from which answers are received means that human beings are in fact open to the infinite. Only the possibility of the infinite can account for the observation that finite humans continue to ask questions and receive answers to them without thereby ceasing to be finite humans. As the infinite horizon of possibilities yields answers to the questions people ask, it remains present only *as* the infinite horizon. By asking questions, persons intend to understand more of this horizon but find that as they do so, it steadily recedes from them. As unrestricted infinite, the horizon is eternally beyond their finitude, ever yielding answers to their questions but never within their grasp.

Persons may be said to transcend the limitations of their existence at a given moment whenever they accept or recognize an answer to a question they have asked. They do not completely transcend such limitations, of course, since, as we have just seen, answered questions give rise to further unanswered ones. But they do transcend those now former limitations by small increments whenever they are no longer bound by the particular restrictions which called forth the question in the first place. The phenomenon of transcendence thus has to do (from the human side) with the self-surpassing nature of knowledge by which persons come to an enhanced understanding of the world by means of answers which come from outside themselves.

We now need to account for the presence and activity of God in this process of enhancement. We shall do this by reflecting upon what it means for a question to be answered. How, that is, is the very ordinary event of answering questions an exemplification of divine activity and divine inspiration?

Thus far we have said that asking questions signals human openness to the infinite as the storehouse of possibilities from which answers are received. Another way to say this is that while there are several possible responses to a given question, only one will be accepted as the satisfactory answer by the questioner.[5] But what is the criterion or yardstick by which that response is chosen as right over other responses, and, more importantly, where is God in all of this?

The most characteristic way of describing the process by which persons select answers from among all possible responses involves noticing that answers are typically chosen when they are seen to be "good." That is, an answer arises from the set of all possible responses when it, more than they, satisfies the notion of goodness which is most appropriate to the context of the question asked by the questioner. Thus, before any specific act of choosing is the concept of goodness which is present to the questioner even if he or she has never consciously thought about it.

In addition to goodness as the ground of the act of questioning, there is also that which all questions intend as their general end, since answers are chosen as answers on the basis of their greater contextual goodness. So goodness is seen to be both the origin and the end of all acts of answered questions; no question could ever be satisfactorily answered without goodness as the criterion.[6]

This analysis holds for all answered questions, not just those which are taken to be morally good.[7] I am not saying that all answers to questions are morally good, but rather that goodness is revealed as the condition for being able to choose any answer at all. It is surely the case that many morally evil answers have been accepted and acted upon in history. What they have in common with morally good answers, however, is that both are chosen from among a larger number of possibilities, with the criterion for choice itself always remaining goodness with respect to a particular goal.

We can now see how God is involved in the process of asking and answering questions and thus in the process of human self-transcendence. One of the most enduring and traditional attributes of God is His goodness: "No one is good but God alone" (Mark 10:18; a closer translation would be "No one is good except the one God").[8] However, the goodness of God is unlike the goodness of anything else, since in all other cases being good is assessed only after comparison against some earlier standard of goodness. Clearly, though, such cannot be the case with God's goodness since nothing exists before God, either logically or chronologically, against which God's character could be tested and assessed as good.[9] So, we cannot say that the meaning of "God is good" is identical to "Jones is good." What must be the case, then, is that "God is good" is what would be meant by the awkward-sounding phrase "God is goodness": the character of God is that by which human beings discriminate between good and evil. What this signifies in turn, with respect to our purposes here, is that whenever human beings choose an answer on the basis of its greater goodness over all other less good responses, what they are concurrently doing, consciously or otherwise, is referring to and depending upon an ultimate measure of goodness, which Christians name God. The character of God as good is affirmed in principle whenever people make choices.

In this brief analysis of the phenomenon of asking and answering questions, we have seen that ultimately all answered questions are grounded in the character of God as the goodness which discriminates between responses and answers. The character of God as good, therefore, stands as the ultimate ground of humans being able to transcend their cognitive finitude incrementally without either ceasing to be finite on the one hand or reducing God simply to another entity in the universe on the other. This is what is meant by saying that God inspires all human acts of understanding; inasmuch as those acts fulfill the need for knowledge to be good or acceptable to the knowing mind, they are ultimately grounded in and thus initiated by God.

It may be objected that this understanding of divine inspiration is unhelpful precisely because all acts of human understanding are seen as divinely inspired. Here I can do no better than cite and defend Rahner's response to the same objection: "Why, then, may this not be the case?"[10] That is, for those persons who insist that God is not simply another entity in the universe, divine activity must be explained carefully so that it is relevantly distinct from the activity of mundane actors and yet remains appropriate to a doctrine of God. Ever since Thomas Aquinas, this has been accomplished by means of the doctrine of secondary causation, a doctrine summarized by Rahner when he says that

> the chain of causality has its basis in [God, although it is not the case] that by his activity he inserts himself as a link in this chain of causes as one cause among them. The chain itself as a whole, and hence the world in its interconnectedness, . . . is the self-revelation of its ground. And he himself is not to be found within this totality as such. For the ground does not appear within what is grounded if it is really the radical and hence the divine ground, and is not [merely] a function in a network of functions.[11]

The understanding of divine inspiration just presented occupies the same *via media* in that it accounts for the presence and character of God as the ground of the possibility of all knowing acts (and not just some of them, which would be an inappropriate restriction upon divine activity) but yet does not make God a direct or empirical participant in any knowing act. Thus, analogous to what was said earlier about God and goodness, one can never say "God taught me something" and mean the same thing as "Jones taught me something. " Rather, God's participation in acts of knowledge is always a mediated participation; it is always possible to come to know something and *not* recognize God's participation in the process. By the same token, it is not only possible but is in fact necessary for faith to be able to see all acts of understanding as grounded in the character of God. In all knowing acts, it is appropriate to recognize and be thankful to God as the indirect and ultimate initiator of understanding. This is what is meant by divine inspiration.

Divine Inspiration and Biblical Inspiration

We have seen how all acts of knowing and understanding are properly grounded in God's good character and thus in what way they can all be said to result from divine inspiration. Such an account shows that all acts of human enhancement or transcendence are really a growth from a less good state to a more good state. The condition of the possibility of any such growth is the existence of God as (among other things) the goodness which all acts of choosing presuppose and the inspiration of God as the activity by which answers are selected as good from among a larger set of possible responses.

However, it is not yet clear how divine inspiration coordinates with biblical inspiration; that is, it is not yet clear how to distinguish the inspiration of the Bible from the inspiration of any other thing. In traditional theories of biblical inspiration this was not a problem in that both were said to terminate in the Bible and were therefore never distinguished. For us, though, the two concepts are very distinct, and we need to discuss their relationship. In what ways is biblical inspiration—a much narrower concept than divine inspiration—related to it? There are four such ways.

The first way in which biblical inspiration is related to divine inspiration is that it is an exemplification of divine inspiration. In other words, we must expect that biblical inspiration will operate in the same psychological manner as do all other acts of enhancement or self-transcendence. All such acts are ultimately initiated by God, not in the sense that God directly causes them "as one cause within the whole chain of causes," but rather in that His character as infinite goodness is the ground of any act of enhancement at all. Thus, when a Christian community confesses its acceptance of biblical inspiration as an aspect of its entire statement of belief in God, it is on one level saying no more than that God operates through the Bible in the same mode that He operates through any other means. The net effect of this observation is (again) that the concept of biblical inspiration by itself cannot account either for the distinctiveness of the Christian message on the one hand or for the singular status of the Bible within the Christian community on the other. Because biblical inspiration is a subset of the larger category of divine inspiration, it is unable per se to ground the distinctiveness of any other part of Christian doctrine, much less the whole of it.

If the singularity or uniqueness of Christianity cannot be grounded in the inspiration of the Bible because, as we have just seen, there is a formal similarity between divine inspiration through the Bible and divine inspiration outside the Bible, then in what does the singularity of Christianity consist, and how is *that* related to the concept of biblical inspiration? My response is that it is the content or material of Christianity which accounts for its singularity, namely, salvation by God through Jesus. "Salvation" is here understood both in its narrower sense of divine forgiveness of human sin and in its wider sense of health, peace, and fullness of life (which is the meaning of the Hebrew *shalom*).[12] The uniqueness of Christianity thus derives from the particular understanding of salvation understood by and experienced within the Christian community: salvation comes from being in a relationship with God, who is the Father of Jesus, who initiates and completes that salvation, and who is the source of all fullness of life. Because this salvation is at the heart of all specifically Christian confessions, any theological reflection upon Christianity not ultimately centered in it is at best only deficiently or ambiguously Christian.

The insistence upon salvation as the ultimate foundation for all Christian experience and reflection leads the way to the second statement of the relationship between divine and biblical inspiration. Biblical inspiration is divine inspiration with respect to salvation through Jesus. Thus, the test for the presence of biblical inspiration is whether an experience of salvation through Jesus in the present is consonant with, and therefore shaped by, salvation as reflected upon in the New Testament.

This statement is not intended to serve as a criterion for distinguishing inspired from noninspired portions of the Bible. Such an understanding presumes that inspiration is a category which refers primarily to words rather than to persons, a presumption which throughout this study I have taken to be invalid. I would instead argue that "biblical inspiration" refers to the believer's confession of being saved and in turn that being saved means living a life which embodies the same love of and unconditional forgiveness toward others that a believer has already received from God through Christ. The phrase "biblical inspiration" is thus an abbreviated reference to "the experience of salvation by God through Christ as mediated through the Bible. " Putting it this way helps us to see again that "biblical inspiration" refers primarily to personal agents rather than primarily to a book. Concurrently, it helps us to see that "evidences of biblical inspiration," far from being literary, logical, or historical-referential in nature, are instead the same as what is meant by "evidences of salvation," that is, a quality of life ultimately characterized by loving and forgiving those who, like ourselves, are not deserving.

The third criterion for relating biblical inspiration to divine inspiration is that biblical inspiration is normative divine inspiration with respect to human salvation. The second criterion focused attention upon certain kinds of enhancing acts, that is, those which reflect upon and mediate God's salvation. This one specifies biblical inspiration even further by insisting that it is only an experience of salvation that can demonstrate consonance with salvation as presented in the Bible which the Christian community will accept as being initiated by God. There have been innumerable ways of thinking about salvation in history, both inside and outside the Christian community. "Biblical inspiration" is the way in which the church accounts for the divine initiation of the experience of salvation, past and present, as well as for the commonality of the shape of that salvation among Christians but not among non-Christians. This is what is meant by normativity: the singularly authoritative status of the Bible within the Christian community as the rule or measure which defines Christian salvation. In order for an experience of salvation to be Christian, it must be consonant with the salvation of believers in the Bible and thus inspired by the God of the Bible whom Christians know and worship as the Father of Jesus. The normative aspect of Christian biblical inspiration thus authorizes certain ways of thinking about salvation, declaring them to be constitutive of the ways God is recognized to have worked in the past and of the ways He may be trusted to work in the present and future.

The fourth and fullest statement relating biblical inspiration to divine inspiration is that biblical inspiration is normative and foundational divine inspiration with respect to human salvation. Whereas the previous aspect of biblical inspiration proposed that certain reflections on salvation *are* normative for the Christian understanding of salvation, this one provides a limit to such authorized accounts of salvation. The limiting factor is essentially chronological in nature: how did the earliest generations of Christian believers experience and understand salvation? However the answers to this question may be characterized, they constitute the norm for all subsequent accounts of salvation, regardless of the possible greater influence which later accounts may have exercised within the Christian community.[13]

The net effect of insisting upon the foundational or chronological aspect of biblical inspiration is to distinguish conceptually between biblical books which have not had much of an influence upon the church and postbiblical works which have.[14] "Christian Scripture" is defined as that which is normative and foundational for the Christian church,[15] and "biblical inspiration" is how the church accounts for the commonality of ways of experiencing God's salvation on the part of Christian believers throughout history.

It can be seen that the fourth criterion of biblical inspiration, involving chronological priority, it but the reverse side of the question of canonization. Canonization refers to the historical process of certain Christian works being brought together to comprise a yardstick or measure (Greek: *kanon*) by which the church would evaluate and regulate the Christianness of salvation. When faced on the one hand with a large and growing corpus of writings by Christian believers and on the other with an increasingly diverse set of practices and doctrines each claiming to be Christian, the church had to articulate criteria by which to distinguish proper from improper expressions of Christianity. As Hans von Campenhausen shows in his masterful *The Formation of the Christian Bible*, however:

> It is purely arbitrary to make liturgical use, or formal definition, or the concept of inspiration, or, worse still, official ecclesiastical confirmation the only criterion . . . of what is canonical. The fundamental idea—in keeping with the word—is the status of a standard or norm which some writing or collection of writings has acquired for faith and life. Its binding character must be universally and definitively recognised. As a result of this the demarcation of the canonical from non-canonical material in the course of time follows to some extent automatically; and because the Canon testifies to the divine revelation, and because

its authority is of divine, not human origin, further reflection attributes it almost at once to a special, direct intervention or inspiration of God.[16]

That is, the criteria by which we most often evaluate the Christianness of given actions or beliefs are not the same ones that the church employed before the formation of a recognized canon, precisely because no such canon existed for it at that time. The criterion for this precanon church was rather the actual authority or influence which a given work exercised in concrete ecclesial situations. (This is what von Campenhausen means by the "binding character" of a writing.) Reflection on the presence of this influence within the Christian community, an influence which drew the attention of the community primarily to God rather than to any human agency, led to the conclusion that God was the ultimate initiator or author of the work, a conclusion known then and now as inspiration.

The notions of foundationality and canonicity bring to mind that issue which has traditionally gone under the name of the "cessation of revelation." (This is an imprecise description since what was meant was not that God ceased all self-revelatory activity but rather that God ceased any qualitatively *new* self-revelatory activity.) The issue arose as a response to the question of why the church does not continue to add materials to its scripture, which is the question of the closing of the canon. Von Campenhausen asserts that the canon was closed primarily because of the influence of Montanists, an enthusiastic (or perhaps charismatic) and apocalyptic sect of the late second and third centuries. The presence of the spirit of prophecy in the Montanists prompted them to treat the New Testament itself as openly as the first generations of Christians had treated the Old, that is, to view it as an intermediary step within the entire sweep of progressive revelation. What this implied, of course, was that the notion of salvation contained within the New Testament was subject to whatever reformulation the spirit of the Montanists might reveal, and it was with respect to this implication both that Montanism was declared an improper choice (i.e., a heresy) and that the impulse to close the canon came into being:

> The critical point beyond which Montanism became a sect is thus not directly connected with their attitude to the Canon; it lies instead in the movement's estimate of its own position in salvation-history, which was of course bound to clash with the concept of a canonical norm. Because the Montanists were not prepared to give up attaching absolute value to the extravagant authority of their spirit and their founding prophets, they necessarily exempted them from any further test. . . . In this way they went behind Christian "beginnings," and thus beyond the Canon which was meant to determine and preserve those beginnings.[17]

Rahner's analysis of the same phenomenon is quite similar, although we should not be surprised that it places more emphasis on the existence of the church (as community of saved persons) than it does on the experience of salvation (perpetuated throughout history in and by the church).[18] His claim is that the church is God's ultimate intention for humankind and that the concept of a church which is fully in possession of God's saving grace, and therefore is no longer in progressive transition toward it, presupposes the concept of a closed canon. Thus, the closure of the canon is not so much to be historically specified as it is to be conceptually and normatively specified: it occurred when the church became that which God had always intended it to become. Rahner's "when" is much more fluid than von Campenhausen's, although his canon itself is not fluid precisely because for him the church actually became what God intended it to become quite early in its history, and the existence of that church is impossible to conceive apart from the existence of a closed, normative canon. Thus, the differences here are in fact less significant than they at first appear and are probably best attributed to the different denominational traditions represented by each as well as to the different interests of historical and systematic theologians.

Of specific interest is the fact that both authors agree that inspiration was attributed to a given text only after its saving influence had been historically recognized and appropriated. The absence of such influence was thus a sufficient indicator of the absence of inspiration. The failure to notice this, coupled with the tendency to make authority consequent upon inspiration, characterizes most of the inspiration theories which this study has criticized.

A Concluding Comment

In this chapter we have discussed the concept of divine inspiration and have introduced four criteria by which to designate biblical inspiration as a subset of divine inspiration. The usefulness of these criteria rests in their relating the narrower concept to the wider one, which allows us to say that both types of inspiration operate in the same formal manner but yet are not identical.

I shall now summarize my theory of biblical inspiration. The phrase "biblical inspiration" initially points not to the Bible but to Christian believers who have experienced salvation from God through the Bible. Since this experience is a saving experience, it is referred to as a self-transcendence whose ultimate initiator is God. Because the emphasis in all acts of divine inspiration is upon God as initiator and humans as recipients, the condition sine qua non of biblical inspiration is salvation by God. To discuss the inspiration of the Bible apart from the context of the saving activity of God is formally as moot as to discuss the inspiration of an artist who has never painted or a teacher who has never had students. All attempts to account for biblical inspiration which fail to rest upon the presence of salvation in the human recipient at best are only ambiguously Christian and at worst ground the specificity of Christianity in such nonreligious concepts as logic, interior feelings, historical accuracy, or the like.

The greatest advantage which I believe attaches to my theory of biblical inspiration is that it does not shift the focus of Christian belief away from the saving presence of God among believers. That is, in order to understand the present concept of inspiration, one does not have to be saved *and* assent to a doctrine of inerrancy, a formal concept of logic, a certain understanding of history, or anything else. The presence of salvation by itself is the sufficient sign of the operation of biblical inspiration, because salvation alone is that which God desires for all persons (1 Timothy 2:4).

At this point, it is appropriate to step back and address the larger question of the aim of this study. It was triggered by the collision of three observations. The first is that the Bible is used authoritatively in the church, the second is that the traditional Christian way to account for this authority has been to say that the Bible is inspired, and the third is that most explanations of this account have been unsuccessful. The first reason is that they characteristically assume that inspiration is a phenomenon which can terminate in a book. The second reason is that they gratuitously confuse talk about the Bible with talk about God, thus unconsciously investing the Bible with characteristics which properly belong only to God. In particular, it is the divine characteristics of comprehensiveness and indeceivability which arise so uncannily in discussions about the Bible. These two reasons, then, constituted the bases for my critical activity in the first two chapters of this book.

William Abraham's work on inspiration helped to locate the weakness of traditional accounts of inspiration by pointing out that acts which are properly called inspired acts have a tripartite rather than a bipartite structure. That is, in any inspired act it is possible to identify an initiating agent, a medium, and a receiving agent. In general, then, an inspired act would be one in which the receiving agent's life is enhanced by the initiating agent by means of the medium in ways which are appropriate to that medium.

Armed with this insight, I then set out to see how biblical inspiration might be construed. Building upon a further hint from Abraham, I began by reflecting upon the third category of the receiving agent; we are more familiar with these agents since in principle, at least, they include ourselves. I determined that biblical inspiration is a mediated enhancement of human existence by God, the Father of Jesus, through the Bible ("through the Bible" here means in conformity with or in dependence upon the Bible). I also proposed that all of the ways that the doctrine of God may be understood, the one which best coordinates with this understanding of inspiration is that offered by the school of transcendental Thomism, which (broadly put) insists that God's acts always be seen as mediated through the world rather than immediately occurring in the world.

Reflection upon this way of construing biblical inspiration led to the observation that only Christians call the Bible inspired in this way. That is, biblical inspiration is not a property of the words or even the message of the Bible per se but is rather the way that Christianly saved persons retrace the route of their salvation from God through the Bible to the actual communities in which they were saved. Thus, the possession of salvation is intrinsic or constitutive to the description, if not also the definition, of biblical inspiration. Put into conceptual terms, it is not the words or message alone which are inspired since words and messages cannot receive inspiration. Only reasoning creatures can receive inspiration. Put into more existential or concrete terms, the words and message of the Bible are only said to be inspired when they are received by the community which they have inspired, that is, when they are read as God's word by that community which God has created through them. Since it is only this saved community (i.e., the church) which confesses the Bible as inspired, the definition of inspiration must include salvation as God's enhancement of human life through the Bible.

There are two potential weaknesses to my proposal. The first is that it simply sounds odd to say that biblical inspiration primarily has to do with Christian salvation rather than properties or characteristics of a book. It seems as though this way of construing inspiration is off the subject much as I accused many other theories of being off the subject in confusing the doctrine of the Bible with the doctrine of God.

I would argue that I do not commit a similar confusion. It is certainly the case that the Christian tradition is accustomed to calling the Bible inspired in what we might call a passive sense, the sense that assumes that the Bible itself receives divine inspiration and then invites us to search for the properties of inspiration within it. But this approach is wrongheaded because it ignores the fact that only the Christianly saved community believes that the Bible is inspired. Properties, on the other hand, are phenomena which are present independent of belief, at least in their usual sense, and are therefore true of the object to which they apply regardless of the belief structure of any particular observer. For example, some properties of the Christian Bible are that it has sixty-six books, two major sections or testaments, several minor sections such as law, prophets, writings, gospels, epistles and apocalyptic, and so on. Because only the Christian community of belief accepts the inspiration of the Bible, however, inspiration is not a belief-independent property like these.

The second and perhaps greater weakness of my proposal is that in denying that inspiration is a property of the Bible itself, it seems to eviscerate most traditional notions of biblical authority (since inspiration functions as the explanation for authority, as noted earlier). That is, the church has traditionally tended to authorize both religious and theological activity from the Bible because of its belief that contact with the Bible is contact with God.[19] Does not my proposal soften or weaken the possibility of such authorization and at least potentially make the community of saved persons (the church) as important as the Bible in authorizing religious and theological activity?

Again, I would argue that the present proposal is not susceptible to this objection. While it is true that the present theory of biblical inspiration brings in the church (as the community of saved persons) in a way that most evangelical theories do not, it is not the case that it brings it in as an equal partner to the Bible, which is what this objection fears. Instead, I would agree in large part with David Kelsey, who argues that the concepts of church and Bible imply each other and thus that neither may adequately be discussed apart from the other. There is no Christian Bible apart from the church, because it is only in the church that the Bible is accepted as Scripture, to use the distinction made in the Introduction. By the same token, there is no church apart from the Bible, because it is only those communities which can show substantial dependence upon the Bible that can claim to be Christian communities.

However, and here I distance myself somewhat from Kelsey, to say that the Bible and the church imply each other does not mean that they are of equal importance, for the concept of church does not include the criterion of foundationality as does the concept of inspired Bible.[20] That is, the mutual implication of Bible and church is an ordered implication. The community of saved persons authorizes its Christian activities with reference to the book through which God called it into existence and continues to sustain it today. To rephrase the ancient dictum, the Bible is *norma normans*, while the church is *norma normata*. This, then, leaves intact the specific ways that the church today uses the Bible authoritatively while preserving my insistence that salvation (and by implication the saved community) be a part of the definition of inspiration.

The genius of the doctrine of biblical inspiration is the insight that the Bible conveys God's saving intention to the world. I have referred to this insight as salvation, for the character of God is to love those who hate Him and relentlessly to pursue those who insist upon being lost. Those persons and communities from whom this insight sprang, and their written products, are properly called inspired by those who presently possess it. Without that original insight and those written products, we would not have that saving knowledge of God which we do have. And without that saving knowledge, the Bible would be just another book.

This leads to a final comment. At the conclusion of Chapter 1 I noted that it is possible to interpret Warfield's "church doctrine of the Bible" in a manner that draws attention to the fact that the effect of inspiration lies in the church rather than in the production or words of the Bible alone. Whether or not this is an appropriate reading of Warfield, it is surely my own position. In Chapter 3, then, we considered three characteristically evangelical ways of describing inspiration, descriptions which were not drawn from the Bible but were and are taken by many evangelicals to be true of the Bible. My willingness to retain these descriptions even while reinterpreting them (or, in the case of inerrancy, rejecting it altogether), however, underscores the same point: biblical inspiration refers to the insights which God brings about in the Christian community which are consistent with salvation as experienced and understood by that community, and not to a unique mode of configuring words on a page. Thus, the very approach of this book on biblical inspiration is an exemplification of the way I see inspiration working. Those who read this study and agree with it will do so because it is consonant with the experience of salvation they have gained in their community, and those who reject this study will do so because it does not illustrate their community's experience of salvation. Oddly enough, however, both groups of readers are doing the same thing. Both groups are showing the ultimate criterion for determining the Christianness of anything: compatibility with salvation as understood by their community. If this conclusion is the sole contribution that this study makes to the evangelical community, I will be happy indeed.

Notes

Introduction

1. James T. Burtchaell, *Catholic Theories of Biblical Inspiration since 1810* (Cambridge: Cambridge University Press, 1969), pp. 279–80.

2. See, for, example Kennith Kantzer, "Unity and Diversity in Evangelical Faith," in David F. Wells and John D. Woodbridge, eds., *The Evangelicals* (Nashville: Abingdon Press, 1975), p. 38; and Robert K. Johnston, *Evangelicals at an Impasse* (Atlanta: John Knox, 1979), p. 3.

3. James D. G. Dunn, *Unity and Diversity in the New Testament: An Inquiry into the Character of Earliest Christianity* (Philadelphia: Westminster, 1977).

Chapter 1

1. William Abraham, *The Divine Inspiration of Holy Scripture* (Oxford: Oxford University Press, 1981), p. 11.

2. Cornelius Van Til, *An Introduction to Systematic Theology* (Philadelphia: Presbyterian and Reformed, 1974), p. 31.

3. Charles Hodge, *Systematic Theology*, 3 vols. (Grand Rapids: Eerdmans, 1977), Vol. I, p. 2. All references are to Volume I unless otherwise noted.

4. Ibid., p. 3.

5. Ibid., p. 10.

6. Ibid., p. 11.

7. Ibid.

8. In his biography of his father, A. A. Hodge notes that the publication of the original seven volumes of the *Systematic Theology* stretched from 1870 to 1872. A. A. Hodge, *The Life of Charles Hodge* (New York: Arno and the *New York Times*, 1969), p. 451.

9. Hodge, *Systematic Theology*, p. 14.

10. Ibid., p. 17.

11. That is, advances in the theory or understanding of knowledge.

12. We will see an example of such openness below when we consider Hodge's treatment of geological evolution.

13. Hodge, *Systematic Theology*, pp. 151–88.

14. Ibid., p. 153.

15. Ibid., p. 154.

16. Ibid.

17. Ibid., p. 155.

18. Ibid.

19. Ibid., p. 158.

20. ". . . [N]o prophecy is a matter of one's own interpretation because no prophecy ever came by the impulse of man, but men moved by the Holy Spirit spoke from God."

21. Hodge, *Systematic Theology*, p. 158.

22. Ibid., pp. 156–57.

23. Ibid., p. 164.

24. Ibid., Vol. III, pp. 245–58

25. Ibid., Vol. II, p. 257.

26. Ibid., Vol. I, p. 163.

27. Ibid., p. 165.

28. Ibid., pp. 164–65.

29. Ibid., pp. 169–72.

30. Quoted in Jack Rogers and Donald McKim, *The Authority and Interpretation of the Bible* (San Francisco: Harper & Row, 1979), p. 288, citing the letter as printed in *The Presbyterian* 48 (January 12, 1878): 9.

31. John Leith, ed., *Creeds of the Church* (Richmond: John Knox, 1963–73), p. 195.

32. Ibid.

33. For a critique of this analysis, see John H. Gerstner, "Warfields's Case for Biblical Inerrancy," in John Warwick Montgomery, ed., *God's Inerrant Word* (Minneapolis: Bethany Fellowship, 1974), pp. 115–42. Gerstner attempts to distinguish between the "proof" that the Bible is the Word of God and the "persuasion of the acceptance" that it is so (p. 117). The distinction is elusive unless one specifies "proof" as (perhaps) logical demonstration and "persuasion" as (perhaps) extralogical certainty, which Gerstner does not do.

34. John Woodbridge objects to the notion that a perceptible shift was introduced at this point by Hodge and later by Warfield. In particular, Woodbridge claims that the framers of the Westminster Confession (1643–1649) distinguished the earliest Greek and Hebrew manuscripts from the original autographs (or "sources") and thus that the importance of the distinction was recognized well before Charles Hodge. John D. Woodbridge, *Biblical Authority* (Grand Rapids: Zondervan, 1982), esp. chaps. VI and VII. This objection, which Woodbridge admits as tentative (p. 115), does not directly challenge the point made here concerning the conceptual difference between viewing biblical authority as inferred from discernibly inerrant autographs on the one hand and recognizing it as a result of the interior work of the Holy Spirit on the other. Regardless of how early in history one encounters the autographs argument, it is just a

different approach to the notion of biblical authority from one which does not depend upon any external or inferential warrants.

35. A. A. Hodge, *The Life*, p. 256.

36. Sandeen notes, "Most twentieth-century Fundamentalists and many twentieth-century historians have mistakenly assumed that Protestantism possessed a strong, fully integrated theology of biblical authority which was attacked by advocates of the higher criticism [but,] as we shall see, no such theology existed before 1850. . . . A systematic theology of . . . the infallibility of the Bible had to be created in the midst of the nineteenth-century controversy." Ernest Sandeen, *The Roots of Fundamentalism* (Grand Rapids: Baker Book House, 1978), p. 106.

37. See Sidney E. Ahlstrom, "The Scottish Philosophy and American Theology," *Church History* 24 (1955): 257–72; and George M. Mavrodes, *Fundamentalism and American Culture* (New York: Oxford University Press, 1980), esp. pp. 16–28 and 110–16.

38. Hodge, *Systematic Theology*, p. 4.

39. Or "enthusiastic"; see Sandeen, *Roots of Fundamentalism*, p. 116.

40. Ibid., p. 9.

41. In a manner of speaking. Mike Parsons notes that John Witherspoon, Scottish immigrant and later president of the College of New Jersey at Princeton, "was probably the first Scot to go to a teaching post in America fully acquainted with [Reid's] work." "Warfield and Scripture," *The Churchman* 91 (1977): 201.

42. Thomas Reid, *Philosophical Works* (Hildesheim: Georg Olms Verlagsbuchhandlung, 1967), Vol. I, p. 440.

43. Rogers and Mckim, *Authority and Interpretation*, p. 291.

44. Abraham, *Divine Inspiration*, p. 15. For a similar evaluation, see Gerstner, "Warfield's Case," p. 115.

45. Sandeen, *Roots of Fundamentalism*, p. 115.

46. A. A. Hodge and B. B. Warfield, *Inspiration*, ed. by Roger Nicole (Grand Rapids: Baker, 1979), p. vii, hereafter cited as Nicole. Both Nicole and Gerstner provide extensive primary and secondary bibliographies concerning Warfield's view of inspiration.

47. Ibid.

48. His inaugural address upon induction to the chair of New Testament Literature and Exegesis, Western Theological Seminary, 1880.

49. In *The International Standard Bible Encyclopaedia*, 5 vols. , ed. by James Orr (Chicago: Howard Severence, 1915), Vol. 3, pp. 1473–83.

50. Nicole, *Inspiration*, p. x.

51. Benjamin Breckenridge Warfield, *The Inspiration and Authority of the Bible*, ed. by Samuel G. Craig (Philadelphia: Presbyterian and Reformed, 1948), p. 210.

In his *The Uses of Scripture in Recent Theology* (Philadelphia: Fortress, 1975), David Kelsey calls attention to the peculiarity of this claim in Warfield's theology. He notes that Warfield believed that inspiration was logically dispensable but that it was also methodologically indispensable (pp. 21–2). It is the former because it could be omitted without damage to any other doctrine, as we just saw. It is also the latter because, given the fact that inspiration is "taught" by Scripture, it is of necessity the basic hermeneutical rule guiding the church's use of Scripture. Kelsey concludes from this that inspiration thus functions for Warfield as "a vast hypothesis . . . like the Copernican theory or the theory of evolution," a conclusion with which I would concur.

52. We will consider below Warfield's subsequent and deliberate qualification of his inductivism.

53. Warfield, *Inspiration and Authority*, p. 206. Thus, the opinion of Gerstner ("Warfield's Case," p. 120) that the beginning point of Warfield's epistemology is "sense experience" is untenable. Significantly, Gerstner does not offer a single citation from Warfield's voluminous writings in support of this claim. Genuine inductivism must have been important for Gerstner in a way that it does not appear to have been for Warfield.

54. Cornelius Van Til thus refers to the "Creator-creature distinction" as fundamental to all Christian hermeneutical activity. See his "Introduction" in Warfield, *Inspiration and Authority*, esp. p. 31.

55. Ibid., p. 80.

56. Parsons criticizes Warfield for his fundamental reorientation of Calvinist theology from theocentricity to anthropocentricity dominated by the "almost hysterical quest for certainty" in religious matters. "Man's need, rather than God's word became the guide in doctrinal formulations" ("Warfield and Scripture," p. 200). This does not seem to be a significant criticism in view of the fact that the necessity of Scripture has traditionally been taken by all Christians to be correlative to the necessity of salvation. One wonders what Calvin's theocentricity would amount to if the human need for salvation were subtracted from it.

57. Warfield, *Inspiration and Authority,* p. 420.

58. Ibid., pp. 420–42.

59. Ibid., p. 173.

60. Ibid., p. 95.

61. A representative repudiation of dictation theories may be found in Nicole, *Inspiration*, p. 19. Nicole notes that Hodge actually penned these words (p. xii), but they are, of course, representative of both authors.

62. Warfield, *Inspiration and Authority*, pp. 131–66.

63. "All scripture is inspired by God and profitable for teaching, for reproof, for correction, and for training in righteousness. . . . "

64. Warfield, *Inspiration and Authority,* pp. 132–33.

65. ". . . [N]o prophecy ever came by the impulse of man, but men moved by the Holy Spirit spoke from God."

66. Warfield, *Inspiration and Authority,* p. 137.

67. Ibid., pp. 421–42, see also Nicole, *Inspiration*, p. 42.

68. Ibid., pp. 150–52. Gerstner ("Warfield's Case," p. 134) admits that Warfield's use of "human" in this and similar texts is "unfortunate" because "the whole 'concursus' concept is against [this docetic notion of Scripture]." Gerstner's apology is vitiated by the fact that Warfield is here presenting his own understanding of "concursus."

69. Ibid., pp. 154–60.

70. See John Calvin, *Institutes*, Bk. I, Ch. VI, Pt. IV: "It is true that all things are actuated by a secret instinct of nature, as though they obeyed the eternal command of God, and that what God has once appointed, appears to proceed from voluntary inclination in the creatures."

71. Warfield, *Inspiration and Authority*, p. 160.

72. This was a position long held by Warfield. See his response to objections made against the article coauthored in 1881 with A. A. Hodge, included as Appendix A in Nicole, *Inspiration*, pp. 73–76.

73. Abraham (*Divine Inspiration*, pp. 36–37) argues persuasively that although Warfield and his contemporaries abandoned the *use* of dictation, they did not abandon the *effects* of dictation, that is, verbal inerrancy and the other divine qualities of the Bible. Thus, "the difference between the two views is just one of terminology. . . . This whole emphasis on words is a carry-over from a dictation theory."

74. For example, *Inspiration and Authority*, pp. 93–94.

75. Sandeen says that the article "Inspiration" by Hodge and Warfield in 1881 "elevated the concept to an especially prominent place" (*Roots of Fundamentalism*, p. 128). Since Warfield's 1880 address to the Western Theological Seminary faculty does not mention the autographs in a context ("Inspiration and Criticism") in which such mention would be expected, it is possible that Charles Hodge, whose 1879 revision of his *Outlines of Theology* included references to the autographs, introduced the concept to him.

76. Thus Woodbridge, *Biblical Authority*, pp. 129–35.

77. Abraham, *Divine Inspiration*, p. 15.

78. Hodge, *Systematic Theology*, p. 170.

79. Nicole, *Inspiration*, p. 41.

80. Which he defines, as Hodge did, as inconsistency among biblical assertions or proven variance with historical or scientific facts (Ibid., pp. 45, 54).

81. "Scripture cannot be broken."

82. This raises the related question of canon formation, which Warfield treats explicitly in a short article, "The Formation of the Canon of the New Testament," written in 1892 and included in *Inspiration and Authority*, pp. 411–16.

83. The mechanism that he employs here is to distinguish between errors and "difficulties," to deny the existence of the former in modern copies (Nicole, *Inspiration*, p. 44), and then to note that the phenomenon of textual criticism implicitly presumes the existence of an authoritative and therefore inerrant autograph (Warfield, *Inspiration and Authority*, pp. 104–05.

84. See above, note 73.

85. Warfield, *Inspiration and Authority*, pp. 106–12.

86. Parsons, "Warfield and Scripture," p. 207; emphasis added. Sandeen writes, "For Charles Hodge's dependence upon the previously acquired biblical reverence, B. B. Warfield substituted the externally verified credibility of the apostles as teachers of doctrine" (*Roots of Fundamentalism*, p. 120).

87. Nicole, *Inspiration*, p. 36.

88. A "serious discrepancy," for example, would be that Job and Ecclesiastes both

deny the possibility of reward and punishment in the afterlife, whereas Pauline and later Gospel texts clearly affirm them as actual.

89. Warfield, *Inspiration and Authority*, p. 118.

90. Ibid., pp. 223–24.

91. Or perhaps overwhelm.

92. Sandeen, *Roots of Fundamentalism*, chap. 10, esp. pp. 253–60.

93. We shall see below that his is a refined sort of inductivism, however.

94. A frequently used phrase and, in addition, the title of one of his *Christianity Today* columns (March 3, 1967), reprinted in John Warwick Montgomery, *The Suicide of Christian Theology* (Minneapolis: Bethany Fellowship, 1971), pp. 356–58. Many of Montgomery's articles have enjoyed multiple publishings under various titles and with slight revisions, a fact which at times causes confusion.

95. A paper delivered to the 20th Annual Convention of the American Scientific Affiliation, August 24, 1965, reprinted in Montgomery, *Suicide,* pp. 267–313.

96. Ibid., p. 271.

97. Ibid., p. 287.

98. Montgomery's familiarity with Wittgenstein comes at least partially from his undergraduate mentor at Cornell, Max Black, whose *A Companion to Wittgenstein's 'Tractatus'* (Ithaca, N.Y.: Cornell University Press, 1964) he calls "an exceedingly valuable work." Ibid., p. 300.

99. Ibid., p. 273.

100. Ibid., p. 274, quoting Black, "The Definition of Scientific Method," in his *Problems of Analysis: Philosophical Essays* (London: Routledge & Kegan Paul, 1954), p. 23.

101. Although illustrations could be given without end, Montgomery cites the example of the discovery by Watson and Crick of the double-helix structure of the DNA molecule. Ibid., pp. 272–73.

102. The imagination suggests what *may* be the case in reality, as is seen in C. S. Pierce's category of abduction: "Abduction is the process of forming an explanatory hypothesis. It is the only logical operation which introduces any new idea." C. S. Pierce, *Collected Papers* (Cambridge, Mass.: Harvard University Press, 1965), Vol. V, para. 171. Montgomery denies, however, that he is in any way committed to Pierce's pragmatic philosophy; see ibid., p. 302.

103. Ibid., p. 276.

104. Ibid.

105. Ibid., p. 287.

106. Ibid., p. 277.

107. Montgomery evaluates this criterion higher than that of predictability per se. He does not say why (ibid., p. 278); perhaps the reason is the one noted above, that theory often exceeds the possibility of experimental verification, even if only temporarily. Thus, no competing theories may claim *predictive* superiority prior to experimental verification.

108. Ibid., p. 278, quoting Ian Ramsey, *Models and Mystery* (London: Oxford University Press, 1964), p. 17.

109. Ibid., pp. 281–82.

110. Montgomery uses "reason" and "logic" synonymously here.

111. Montgomery is wrong here concerning the informative status of logical tautologies. Tautologies are empty only to those who already know them as tautologies, or those who know the identical referents of the subject and predicate. Think, though, of the net increase in knowledge of the person who reads the sentence "Barefoot boys do not wear shoes" and does *not* yet know the meaning of "barefoot."

112. Montgomery, "Theologian's Craft," p. 282.

113. The naturalist fallacy is what philosophers call the confusion that argues that because something *is* the case, it *ought* to be the case. An example of the naturalist fallacy often surfaces within Roman Catholic discussions concerning contraception. Some Catholics argue that because sexual intercourse does lead to conception, it ought to lead to conception, that is, it ought not be impeded by artificial contraceptive devices. Those who reject this argument often do so by asking where the "ought" comes from. Their argument is, granted that intercourse *does* lead to conception, why *ought* it lead to conception? If the "ought" is derived solely from the act itself, then it would seem that any act can be justified by the mere occurrence of it, a conclusion which no one wishes to apply to the case of murder, for example. Curiously, Catholic apologists do not seem to see that the same reasoning also *justifies* the use of contraceptives.

114. Montgomery, "Theologian's Craft," pp. 282–83, citing Paul Tillich, *Systematic Theology* (Chicago: University of Chicago Press, 1951), Vol. I, p. 40.

115. Ibid., p. 281.

116. Ibid.

117. Ibid., p. 283.

118. Alvin Plantinga adds "basic beliefs" to the foundation; see Chapter 2, note 2, herein.

119. Montgomery, "Theologian's Craft," p. 283.

120. Ibid., pp. 285–87.

121. Ibid., p. 283.

122. Ibid.

123. John Warwick Montgomery, *The Shape of the Past: An Introduction to Philosophical Historiography* (Ann Arbor: Edwards Brothers, 1963), p. 139f.

124. John Warwick Montgomery, "Clark's Philosophy of History," in Ronald H. Nash, ed., *The Philosophy of Gordon Clark* (Philadelphia: Presbyterian and Reformed, 1968), p. 388.

125. For Hick's presentation of "eschatological verification" and objections raised against it by Kai Nielsen and George Mavrodes, see Malcolm Diamond and Thomas Litzenburg, Jr. , eds., *The Logic of God: Theology and Verification* (Indianapolis: Bobbs-Merrill, 1975), pp. 179–243. For a conceptual repudiation of all future-oriented verification schemes, see Brand Blanshard, *Reason and Analysis* (LaSalle, Ill.: Open Court, 1973), pp. 207–08.

126. See, for example, Willi Marxsen's *The Resurrection of Jesus of Nazareth* (Philadelphia: Westminster, 1979), esp. chap. 2, which challenges the view of the New Testament narratives as accounts of Jesus's *bodily* resurrection and shows as well the irreducible diversity of all five accounts when compared side by side.

127. Clearly Montgomery means for the "if" to be read as "since," but this then becomes a confession of faith and not a straightforward empirical observation.

128. A further unresolved question is how the mind distinguishes between "data" and "norms" in what it encounters in the Scripture. Montgomery gives no clue to an answer here.

129. See p. 30 herein.

130. However, his refusal to include "faith" as one of those elements calling for empirical or inductive analysis is, at best, puzzling; see above, p. 32.

131. It is not claimed that he at all times and in all places reflects them accurately, however. For example, he borrows Ian Ramsey's shoe-foot analogy but curiously rejects the reason for which Ramsey pressed it into service. Ramsey's point is that Christian theories, or doctrines, are counted successful as they account for the lives lived by Christians. He has thus been called a personalist empiricist, which means that his theology primarily attempts to account for the actual shape of a believer's life rather than primarily intending to form it. His theology is more descriptive than it is normative. See Terrence Tilley's 1976 Ph.D. dissertation for the Graduate Theological Union in Berkeley, California, entitled "On Being Tentative in Theology: The Thought of Ian T. Ramsey," where he notes Ramsey's claim that "[religious] language arises from experience—and experience is never purely subjective—and thus has a referent" (p. 123). Nor does Montgomery seem to appreciate the significance of the difference between Ludwig Wittgenstein's earlier *Tractatus Logico-Philsophicus* and later *Philosophical Investigations*. As Anthony Thiselton notes in his analysis of Wittgenstein's influence on philosophical hermeneutics, in the *Tractatus* the conclusion was "that all meaning must be determinate and exact" because meaning is expressed in elementary propositions which themselves reflect simply objects. *The Two Horizons: New Testament Hermeneutics and Philosophical Description* (Grand Rapids: Eerdmans, 1980), p. 378. The later work, though "consists in showing how changes of linguistic surroundings affect particular concepts" or propositions; thus, that their meaning is largely, but not entirely, relative to the context in which they are made (p. 375). Thiselton also notes that the difference between the two outlooks can be characterized by Wittgenstein's moving away from "a sharp dualism between fact and value" and toward the unity of "human life in all its variety and complexity" (p. 39). Montgomery, not surprisingly, quotes approvingly from the earlier *Tractatus* ("the sense of the world must lie outside the world," 6.41) to validate his claim that religious certainty is located outside of the human subject: "Absolute truth and eternal value, if they exist at all, must take their origin from outside the flux of the human situation." Montgomery, *Suicide*, p. 365.

132. The article most directly relevant to this examination has been published in three different places, each time with minor revisions: "Inspiration and Inerrancy: A New Departure," *The Evangelical Theological Society Bulletin*, Spring 1965; *Crisis in Lutheran Theology*, Vol. 1 (Grand Rapids: Baker, 1967), pp. 15–44; and *Suicide*, pp. 314–55. I have used the last source.

133. Montgomery, *Suicide*, p. 314, referring to James Orr, *The Progress of Dogma*, 4th ed. (London: Hodder & Stoughton, 1901).

134. Ibid.

135. Ibid., p. 317.

136. Ibid., p. 323.

137. Ibid.

138. Ibid., p. 324.

139. Ibid., p. 326, quoting A. J. Ayer, *Language, Truth and Logic,* 1st ed. (New York: Dover, 1936), p. 35. The significance of quoting from the first edition will be addressed below. Note: sentences are language-bound entities which express propositions, which themselves are taken to be accurate or at least testable descriptions of the real world. Hence, for example, the following two sentences are said to express the same basic proposition: "Snow is white" and "Der Schnee ist weiss." An obvious problem with this analysis arises when one attempts to specify a particular proposition without using any language to do so, which is a necessary and not merely optional activity if one intends to determine whether the proposition expresses a *true* description of the real world.

140. Ibid., p. 335.

141. Thiselton (*Two Horizons,* p. 39) says that "Bultmann's assumption [is] that speech about God must entail speech about man if it is to acquire and retain an adequate currency of meaning."

142. Montgomery, *Suicide,* p. 346.

143. Ayer later softened his verifiability principle to try to account for the conceptual problems entailed by the early statement of it; see Blanshard, *Reason and Analysis,* chap. 5, for an excellent discussion.

144. See, for example, Tilley, "On Being Tentative," pp. 9–12. Montgomery replies that the verifiability principle is an "explication . . . which itself is neither true nor false." *Suicide,* pp. 352–53, citing Carl Hempel's "The Empiricist Criterion of Meaning," *Revue Internationale de Philosophie* IV (1950). But a sentence itself neither true nor false is hardly acceptable as a criterion for meaningfulness, since the purpose of the criterion is to distinguish true from false.

145. Donald D. Evans, *The Logic of Self-Involvement* (London: SCM Press, 1963), p. 11.

146. While it is true that fundamentalists are characteristically separatist or sectarian in their doctrine of the church, it should not be assumed that they avoid interaction with nonfundamentalists altogether. This is especially evident when one notices the schools and colleges attended by fundamentalists. See Rudolph L. Nelson, "Fundamentalism at Harvard: The Case of Edward John Carnell," *Quarterly Review* 2 (1982): 79–98. (I will question Nelson's designation of Carnell as a fundamentalist below; see note 174.) For a broader survey of the educational orientation of fundamentalism and evangelicalism, see Joel A. Carpenter, "Fundamentalist Institutions and the Rise of Evangelical Protestantism, 1929–1942," *Church History* 49 (1980): 62–75. Carpenter notes the lively expansionist tendencies of fundamentalism in four areas of activity: urban educational institutions, summer Bible conferences, radio broadcasting, and foreign missions.

147. Edward John Carnell, *An Introduction to Christian Apologetics: A Philosophic Defense of Trinitarian-Theistic Faith* (Grand Rapids: Eerdmans, 1948).

148. The *Apologetics* is not Carnell's final word concerning the warrants for Christian truth claims. In particular, a later work, *Christian Commitment: An Apologetic* (New York: Macmillan, 1957), constitutes a substantial reworking of many of the

themes addressed in the *Apologetics*. In choosing to study "the early Carnell," I am therefore deliberately restricting myself to the deductivist Carnell, well aware that he later criticizes his own earlier approach.

149. Carnell, *Apologetics*, p. 23.

150. Ibid., p. 103.

151. Ibid., pp. 104–05.

152. Ibid., p. 106.

153. Ibid., p. 56.

154. Ibid., p. 57.

155. Ibid., p. 59.

156. Ibid.

157. Ibid.

158. Ibid., pp. 45–46.

159. Ibid., p. 46.

160. Ibid., p. 47.

161. Ibid., p. 63.

162. Meaning is defined as "what the mind entertains when it passes judgment upon the facts," ibid., p. 213.

163. Ibid., p. 57.

164. Ibid., p. 62.

165. The later Carnell recognizes the significance of the analysis that all knowledge rests upon judgment (in this case, the judgment concerning the exhaustive applicability of the law of contradiction) rather than upon the law of contradiction itself. The earlier Carnell, however, missed this critical distinction.

166. Note the similarity here with Ayer's understanding of "proposition"; note 139, above.

167. Carnell, *Apologetics*, p. 106.

168. Thales claimed that water was the material cause of all things, a claim which Anaximander refuted by pointing to the existence of fire as an element which water could not produce; see ibid., p. 107.

169. Ibid.

170. Ibid.; emphasis added.

171. Carnell affirms this interpretation of his work when he considers the moral certainty of Christianity. He describes "perfect coherence" as "that state in which symbols are so related one to another, that failure to affirm it involves one in self-contradiction, as in mathematics, geometry, and formal logic. . . . Not to act upon the strength of coherence, or to attempt to do so, is to flee in the face of what the intellect reports to be true, in which case the act is immoral." Ibid., pp. 117–18.

172. Ibid., p. 110. This brief mention of inspiration is located within the larger chapter concerning the criteria of verification in Christianity.

173. Ibid.

174. Ibid., pp. 191–210. Carnell here refers to traditional theology as fundamentalism and to himself as a fundamentalist. Because this book distinguishes between fundamentalism and evangelicalism, and because Carnell fits the profile of the latter, I shall not follow his designation here. The reader is referred to the essay "Orthodoxy: Cultic vs. Classical" for the later Carnell's distinction between traditional Protestants

who are and are not "separatist" in nature as determined by their ecclesiology, and his criticism of such separatism. This is precisely the criterion I have adopted to distinguish fundamentalists from evangelicals. See Ronald H. Nash, ed., *The Case for Biblical Christianity* (Grand Rapids: Eerdmans, 1969), pp. 40–47, esp. p. 42. Carnell's article was originally published in *The Christian Century,* March 30, 1960. I shall only examine his treatment of "lower" criticism because of its relevance to the acts of the knowing mind.

175. Ibid., p. 199.

176. Ibid.

177. Ibid., p. 200.

178. Carnell explicitly affirms that his approach is a priori or "rationalistic," and he does so because of his insistence upon the doctrine of God as the only legitimate starting point for theology and epistemology. See Chapter IX in his *Apologetics,* which he begins by affirming Gordon Clark's statement that "instead of beginning with the facts and later discovering God, unless a thinker begins with God, he can never end with God, or get the facts either," citing Clark, *A Christian Philosophy of Education* (Grand Rapids: Eerdmans, 1946), p. 38.

179. This is precisely the interpretation of Warfield offered by David Kelsey in *Uses of Scripture,* pp. 23–24.

Chapter 2

1. Carl F. H. Henry, *Personal Idealism and Strong's Theology* (Wheaton, Ill.: Van Kampen, 1951), p. 11. The other three are William Newton Clarke, Alvah Hovey, and George W. Northrup.

2. A. H. Strong, *Systematic Theology* (Old Tappan, N.J.: Fleming H. Revell, 1907), p. 3. Interestingly, these are later paralleled by Alvin Plantinga's list of "properly basic beliefs," that is, beliefs which are utterly reasonable to hold but with respect to which no inductive evidence is possible or necessary. His list includes "perceptual beliefs, memory beliefs, beliefs ascribing mental states to other persons," and belief in God; see Alvin Plantinga, "The Reformed Objection to Natural Theology," *Christian Scholar's Review* 11 (1982): 187–98; and "The Reformed Objection Revisited," *Christian Scholar's Review* 12 (1982): esp. 57.

3. Ibid.

4. Ibid., pp. 3–4.

5. Ibid., p. 10.

6. Ibid., p. 7.

7. Ibid., p. 10.

8. John Henry Newman makes the distinction here between "'certitude" and "certainty" respectively. See John Henry Newman, *An Essay in Aid of a Grammar of Assent* (Notre Dame: University of Notre Dame Press, 1979), esp. pp. 173–77; and the excellent review and critique offered by H. Francis Davis, "Newman on Faith and Personal Certitude," *Journal of Theological Studies* ns 12 (1961): 248–59.

9. Strong, *Systematic Theology,* p. 111.

10. Ibid.

11. Ibid. pp. 196–242.

12. Ibid.

13. Ibid., p. 197.

14. Ibid., p. 201.

15. Ibid., pp. 201–02. This is echoed by Peter Stuhlmacher's proposed "hermeneutics of consent"; see Peter Stuhlmacher, *Historical Criticism and Theological Interpretation of Scripture* (Philadelphia: Fortress, 1977), esp. pp. 83–91.

16. Ibid., p. 212.

17. Ibid.

18. A. H. Strong, *Philosophy and Religion* (New York: A. C. Armstrong and Son, 1888), p. 150.

19. Thus, Henry, *Personal Idealism,* p. 70, commenting on the article cited ibid.

20. Strong, *Systematic Theology,* p. 211.

21. A different or additional set of phenomena might also be present, for Strong is careful to deny theories of inspiration which are *merely* natural, especially "intuition" and "illumination" theories; see ibid., pp. 202–8. The point here is that, at the very least, the natural cognitive abilities are fully present and functioning.

22. Ibid., p. 218.

23. Or at least tangential.

24. Strong, *Systematic Theology,* p. 215.

25. Ibid., p. 217.

26. Ibid., p. 219. Strong had earlier defined rationalism as the opposite epistemic tendency, "ignoring the necessity of a holy affection as the *condition* of all right reason in religious things" (p. 30, emphasis added).

27. Errors in science, history, morality, reasoning, Old Testament citations and interpretation, prophecy, the canonicity of certain books, alleged authorship, the religious appropriateness of certain narratives, and the alleged denial by some biblical writers of their own or others' inspiration; ibid., pp. 222–42.

28. Ibid., p. 228.

29. Ibid., p. 229. Although he not only had access to the works of the Princetonians but in fact quoted them several times in his discussion of inspiration (e.g., pp. 198, 211, 217, 227), he did not even mention them in his discussion of the autographs.

30. See, for example, ibid., p. 215–16.

31. This is what Strong meant in the sentence quoted above: "[The Bible is] a witness which proves its divine origin by awakening in us experiences similar to those which it describes, and which are beyond the power of man to originate."

32. See James Barr, *Fundamentalism* (Philadelphia: Westminster, 1977–78), pp. 279–84. The argument here is that all discussions of the apologetic significance of the autographs are meaningless since it is in principle impossible to distinguish an autograph from a copy of one.

33. See Abraham, *The Divine Inspiration of Holy Scripture* (Oxford: Oxford University Press, 1981), p. 94.

34. Tilley, *Talking of God* (New York: Paulist, 1978), p. 72.

35. Strong, *Systematic Theology,* p. 118. A similar statement appears in the section "Proof of Inspiration," p. 201.

36. Ibid., pp. 129–30.

37. Ibid., pp. 118–19.

38. This type of evidence operates cumulatively, not demonstrably, for Strong; see ibid., p. 71.

39. Ibid., p. 123; emphasis added.

40. Strong thus also argues that the only validity of any of the various "proofs of God's existence" is their testimony to, rather than demonstration of, the Being whose existence is the presupposition of all reasoning. "Evidently that which is presupposed in all reasoning cannot itself be proved by reasoning" (ibid., p. 66).

41. Ibid., p. 123.

42. A. H. Strong, *Christ in Creation and Ethical Monism* (Philadelphia: Griffith and Rowland, 1899), p. 2.

43. Strong, *Systematic Theology*, p. 211.

44. With the possible exception of William Sanday's 1893 Bampton Lectures, in *Inspiration* (London: Longmans, Green and Co., 1903). Abraham, however, notes the difficulty which interpreters have had in determining exactly what Sanday intended to say; *Divine Inspiration*, p. 47.

45. Strong, *Systematic Theology*, p. 215.

46. Bernard Ramm, *After Fundamentalism: The Future of Evangelical Theology* (San Francisco: Harper & Row, 1982).

47. Bernard Ramm, *Special Revelation and the Word of God* (Grand Rapids: Eerdmans, 1961).

48. Ibid., p. 175.

49. See, for example, his critique of "the critic and the rationalistic fundamentalist," both of whom view the Bible as a record of divine salvation rather than as a witness to it. He rejects this view because, according to it, "[besides] the Scriptures we would need an elaborate filing system in which every fact or datum mentioned in Scripture would have its authoritative documentation" (ibid., p. 98).

Paradoxically, although Ramm does not directly say it, a valid inference from this view is that the more one concentrates on Scripture itself rather than on that to which it witnesses, the less normative Scripture becomes. That is, if the normative value of Scripture lies in its witness to the saving God, and thus lies outside of itself, then that normative value is decreased to the degree that readers focus their attention upon it rather than upon the saving God. If Scripture is in fact a means but is instead treated as an end, then its normativity as a means is lost.

50. Ibid., p. 71.

51. Ibid., p. 70.

52. Ibid., p. 176.

53. Ibid.

54. Ibid., pp. 59–60.

55. Ibid., p. 87.

56. Ibid., p. 68.

57. See ibid., section 20, pp. 167–75, entitled "Special revelation and the process of its inscripturation."

58. Ibid., p. 170, citing Engelland, "Schrift und Tradition," *Theologische Literaturzeitung* 85 (1960): 22.

59. Ibid., pp. 172–75.

60. Ibid., p. 176.

61. Ibid., p. 175.

62. In *Protestant Biblical Interpretation* (Grand Rapids: Baker, 1970), Ramm affirms this view: "Because historic Protestantism accepts the plenary inspiration of Scripture certain over-all attitudes characterize it. . . . It *approaches* the Bible from the spiritual dimension of faith, trust, prayer and piety"; p. 95; emphasis added.

63. The closest Ramm himself comes to suggesting this identity is in *Revelation*, p. 176. Here he notes the beginnings of a modern resurgence of theological interest in inspiration. The lack of such interest "is hardly a virtue," he says, "as *something must be said* of the relationship of Scripture to revelation, and what is said is the functional equivalent of a doctrine of inspiration." My claim here, then, is that the doctrine of the *testimonium* is the description of how Scripture and revelation are related.

64. Bernard Ramm, *The Witness of the Spirit: An Essay on the Contemporary Relevance of the Internal Witness of the Holy Spirit* (Grand Rapids: Eerdmans, 1959), p. 11.

65. Of Calvin's day.

66. Ramm, *Witness of the Spirit,* p. 12.

67. Ibid., p. 19.

68. Ibid., p. 88.

69. Ibid., p. 93.

70. Ibid., p. 94.

71. Ibid., pp. 39–41.

72. Ramm here cites Aristotle's *Rhetoric* I, 15, as discussed by H. Strathman, "Martus, etc.," *Theological Dictionary of the New Testament* (Grand Rapids: Eerdmans, 1974), Vol. IV, p. 478.

73. Ramm, *Witness of the Spirit,* p. 95.

74. Ibid., p. 96.

75. Traditionally, Protestant systematic theologians have understood faith in three ways, all of which must be present for faith to be saving faith. Heinrich Heppe distinguishes them as *notitia, assensus,* and *fiducia.* The first two are properties of the knowing mind, and the latter is a property of the will. See Heinrich Heppe, *Reformed Dogmatics* (Grand Rapids: Baker, 1978), p. 530.

76. Ramm, *Witness of the Spirit,* pp. 96–97, quoting Vincent Taylor, *The Names of Jesus* (London: Macmillan, 1959), p. 51.

77. Ibid., p. 97.

78. The reader will notice the similarity between this analysis of the persuasiveness of truth and that of the Second Vatican Council's document on religious freedom ("Dignitatis Humanae"): "The truth cannot impose itself except by virtue of its own truth, as it makes its entrance into the mind at once quietly and with power. . . . [Persons] are . . . bound to adhere to the truth, once it is known, and to order their whole lives in accord with the demands of truth." See Walter M. Abbott, S. J. , ed., *The Documents of Vatican II* (New York: Guild, 1966), pp. 677, 679.

79. Ramm, *Witness of the Spirit,* p. 94.

80. William J. Abraham, *The Divine Inspiration of Holy Scripture* (London: Oxford University Press, 1981).

81. He is, of course, conversant with other evangelical traditions; we have already encountered him in our consideration of B. B. Warfield. He does not claim that the Wesleyan tradition has influenced his concept of inspiration in ways peculiar to Wesleyanism, and neither do I. His value as a Wesleyan, therefore, is in illustrating the transdenominational character of evangelicalism which this study takes as a constituent in the definition of evangelicalism.

82. In particular, we saw the blurring of this distinction in Montgomery, who grounds the truthfulness of all biblical assertions on the datum: "If Christ is God, then He speaks the truth concerning the . . . Old Testament and of the . . . New Testament. . . . It follows . . . that all biblical assertions . . . are to be regarded as revealed truth." As Ramm points outs, this approach confuses "content" and "acceptance of content." It also assumes gratuitously that inspiration requires inerrancy.

83. In an unpublished review of Paul Achtemeier's *The Inspiration of Scripture* (Philadelphia: Westminster, 1980), Abraham writes with respect to divine activity in inspiration: "At this point there is no alternative, in my view, to going back and covering the ground so marvelously opened up by Aquinas and his doctrine of analogy and so judiciously illuminated by the extensive work on religious language inspired by Wittgenstein." Abraham does not, however, cite any Thomistic sources in *Divine Inspiration*. Part of my critique of him will be that his work is incomplete in just those areas where contemporary Thomists have been most productive.

84. Abraham, *Divine Inspiration*, pp. 7, 9.

85. Abraham notes that all evangelical theories, regardless of other differences, are united in their use of the term "plenary" (or "verbal") inspiration. What this term intends to signal, he says, is that divine inspiration is a property of the words of Scripture, though not necessarily a result of mechanistic dictation on the part of God. Plenary inspiration thus rejects immediate divine intervention at the point of the writing of Scripture. It also allows for stylistic differences by a process whose description by Abraham is essentially that which is usually called divine providence; see ibid., p. 4. Not all would agree with this account of plenary inspiration. For example, Warfield accepted immediate divine intervention at the point of the writing of Scripture, and he is deliberate in using the word "plenary" to refer to his account of inspiration.

86. Ibid., p. 37.

87. The major problem is that regardless of how energetically evangelicals reject dictation as the mode of inspiration, they end up accepting it under another name when they confuse inspiration with speaking; see Chapter 1, note 73, herein.

88. Abraham, *Divine Inspiration*, pp. 63, 61. The reader here begins to notice Abraham's appreciation of Thomas, especially that interpretation of Thomas offered by the so-called school of transcendental Thomists. Since the last chapter will consider transcendental Thomism in more detail, I shall not pause to address it here except to note the affinity between Abraham's quote and the method of philosophical inquiry summarized as "coming to understand by grasping the proportionate likenesses among examples" by David Burrell in *Exercises in Religious Understanding* (Notre Dame: University of Notre Dame Press, 1974), pp. 4–5.

89. Ibid., p. 62.

90. Ibid., chap. 3, "The Concept of Inspiration," pp. 63–75.

91. Philosophers of language would say that the enriching of one's learning faculties is "analytic" to the concept of inspiration. What is analytic to a concept is that which is necessary for its proper meaning and use and in whose absence one is not talking of the same concept. Although it is often difficult to specify all of the analytic elements of a concept, it is not difficult to specify individual ones. Abraham does not claim that his paradigm illustrates all necessary members of the concept of inspiration, but only that the ones he lists are necessary members.

92. The similarity of Abraham's language here with explicitly sacramental language ought not be overlooked. Lutherans, for example, have traditionally insisted on using the prepositions, "in, with, and under . . . to designate the presence of the body [and blood] of Christ in the Lord's Supper." Francis Pieper, *Christian Dogmatics* (St. Louis: Concordia, 1953), Vol. III, p. 345; see pp. 353–64 for a fuller explanation. This linguistic usage illustrates the claim that the Bible is a sacrament and that faith must be present in the readers of the Bible in order for it to be apprehended as the medium of God's self-revelation. The negative significance of this claim is that deductivist theories of inspiration ignore the sacramental aspect of Scripture when they insist upon discernible manifestations of divinity such as the inerrancy of the text itself.

93. This is surely what Abraham had in mind when he spoke about the "work on religious language inspired by Wittgenstein," note 83, above.

94. Thus, with respect to the example cited above in Chapter 1, note 88, a discernible degree of difference exists between Job and Ecclesiastes on the one hand and Wisdom of Solomon, Paul, and Revelation on the other concerning the concept of reward in the afterlife. According to my criterion, it is the latter view which on historical grounds is seen to be "inspired," because that view has shaped the church's understanding of the afterlife while the former has not. This raises the question, which strictly speaking is tangential to the topic of this study, of "progressive revelation." Evangelicals have understood progressive revelation as that which accounts for the "internal organic development" of the doctrines of Christian faith (see Charles Hodge, *Systematic Theology*, pp. 446–47). But this is simply a recognition of the fact that not all biblical authors say the same thing about the same subject, as in the case of postdeath retribution. Hodge's discussion, to be sure, presumes that the development occurs within the limits of *logical* consistency: "All that is in a full-grown tree was potentially in the seed." What is important to notice with respect to the concept of progressive revelation, though, is that its sole usefulness is its ability to account for existing discernible differences. Were there no such differences exhibited within the Bible, "progressive revelation" would not be needed to account for them.

95. In *Exercises*, Burrell illustrates the same point in his discussion of the peculiar way in which God is said to be good according to Thomas in *Summa Theologiae*, Book I, Questions 5a, b. The usual assessment or evaluation of goodness cannot apply to God, since "P is good" implies a standard of goodness which exists logically prior to P, and nothing exists prior to God. Therefore, "God is good" can only mean that God is the one whose existence is the condition for our being attracted or drawn to whatever it is that we assess as good. The specific illustration is of a person "thanking us for everything we did for him, when we were conscious simply of doing what was ours to do. He might retort to our disclaimer: so much the better; you are an immense

help to me just by being around and being yourself. . . . In this sense, then, God's being good is more like his being utterly desirable because he is so much himself, so much his own being that his very presence promises to help put me in touch with mine." *Exercises*, p. 111. This serves neatly as an illustration of a noninformative case of inspiration, although it is not claimed that Burrell intended it as such.

96. For example, the model of the speaking prophet in Hodge and Warfield, the model of historical consistency in Montgomery, and the model of logical consistency in Carnell.

97. In the same way, for example, that believers and unbelievers alike are equally able to discern instances of historical discrepancies, logical inconsistencies, and the like.

98. Burrell comments with respect to Thomas: "Aquinas' mode of inquiry offers a therapy specifically designed for anyone whose *interest* in things divine tends to turn those things into questions." *Exercises*, p. 136. Ian T. Ramsey makes the same point: "We shall only take up a theological standpoint towards the universe if we have a questioning mind, which pursues its questions until there breaks in on us a situation which is characterized by depth, wonderment, and so on." *Religious Language: An Empirical Placing of Theological Phrases* (London: SCM, 1963), pp. 86–7.

99. Ibid., p. 11.

100. Ibid., p. 75.

101. See the article "Hermeneutics" by Raymond Brown in *Jerome Biblical Commentary*, especially 71:66, where he says, "To decide from a philosophical theory of instrumentality what God could and could not have done in inspiring scripture is risky. . . . It is far better to work *a posteriori*: to see what God has done and then to formulate a theory that can account for it."

Chapter 3

1. See, for example, the different meanings to be derived from the different order given to the cleansing of the Temple by Matthew and Mark. Mark intentionally locates the Temple story inside the story of the cursing of the fig tree, thereby alerting his readers that neither story may be understood apart from the other (Mark 11:12–25). Matthew, on the other hand, dissociates these stories in his narrative (Matthew 21:12–22). Regardless of which of these accounts (if either) accurately reflects "what happened," it is clear that the meaning for the evangelist and the reader is located in the narrative structure and not in the bare events themselves.

2. Abraham, *The Divine Inspiration of Holy Scripture* (Oxford: Oxford University Press, 1981), p. 6. Thomas A. Hoffman, S.J., notes the same uneasiness concerning inspiration within the Roman Catholic tradition. See his excellent article "Inspiration, Normativeness, Canonicity, and the Unique Sacred Character of the Bible," *Catholic Biblical Quarterly* 44 (1982): 447–69, which begins with the sentence "The doctrine of biblical inspiration . . . has come upon hard times."

3. R. Hooykas attempts to do the same thing in his *Religion and the Rise of Modern Science* (Grand Rapids: Eerdmans, 1978), but from the discipline of science rather than theology.

4. I am not ignoring my criticism of the inductivism of Hodge, Warfield, et al. The

point here is that they believed that they were being faithful to the inductive approach, and they utilized it because they recognized its success in the natural sciences.

5. In addition to the Montgomery discussion above, see Francis Schaeffer, *The God Who Is There* (Downers Grove, Ill.: Inter-Varsity, 1970); *Two Contents, Two Realities* (Downers Grove, Ill.: Inter-Varsity, 1974); and especially *No Final Conflict: The Bible Without Error in All That It Affirms* (Downers Grove, Ill.: Inter-Varsity, 1970). See also Harold Lindsell's *The Battle for the Bible* (Grand Rapids: Zondervan, 1976).

6. The reader is cautioned to distinguish between the inspiration of the Bible and talk of the inspiration of the Bible. In conceptual terms, the distinction is between first-order and second-order activities, or experience and reflection. This is what James Burtchaell means when he laments, "Most inspiration theory has not been talk about the Bible. It has been talk about talk about the Bible"; see his *Catholic Theories of Biblical Inspiration since 1810* (Cambridge: Cambridge University Press, 1969), p. 283.

7. We have already referred to Thiselton's *The Two Horizons* in the consideration of Montgomery. See also Gerald Sheppard, "Biblical Hermeneutics: The Academic Language of Evangelical Indentity," *Union Quarterly Seminary Review* 32 (1977): 81–94; and "Recovering the Natural Sense" *Theology Today* 38 (1981): 330–37.

8. *Christianity Today* is a journal which is frequently read and cited by evangelicals and within which issues of current interest to evangelicals are usually brought to light. Its own self-description is that it is "a magazine of evangelical commitment." In a recent issue, the journal "rejoined the origins debate" and rendered a cautious and qualified acceptance of various geological-cosmological conclusions traditionally represented more by the evolutionists than by the creationists in the ongoing American debate. Such an openness to positions previously resisted by the journal, coupled with a vigorous exchange within the particular issue itself, is evidence of the relative flexibility of evangelicalism which distinguishes it from Protestant fundamentalism. See *Christianity Today* 26 (8 October 1982): 22–45.

9. To say that the point of creature language is to situate persons vertically and horizontally is to affirm, not deny, the importance of cosmogony and related fields of study. This study simply chooses to discuss a particular aspect of cosmogony, namely, its theological implications.

10. More will be said about this transcendental relationship in Chapter 5.

11. That is, between animals and humans.

12. The obverse of this realization—that animals have rights in human society which in the nature of the case only humans can recognize and enforce—is growing at present as well. See Peter Singer's groundbreaking *Animal Liberation* (New York: Avon, 1975).

13. Special exceptions to this generalization, such as oppression, insanity, and the like, do not obviate it.

14. This is because "responsibility" analytically entails "responsibility to someone or something external." I shall address this in more detail in Chapter 5.

15. This asymmetricality may be seen quite clearly if we take the time to analyze the concept of "invitation" which is, I would claim, the best way to construe the nature

of God's self-presentation to human beings. In any invitation there are two categories or parties involved: the inviter and the invitee. The latter category may be further divided into those who accept the invitation and those who reject it. Those who accept the invitation will end up at, say, the dinner party. The ultimate responsibility for their being there will be the inviter's and not their own, since they would not be there apart from the invitation by the inviter. Their responsibility is secondary to the inviter's. Those who reject the invitation will not end up at the dinner party, and thus the ultimate responsibility for their not being there *will* be their own, since clearly the inviter wanted them to attend. Here their responsibility takes precedence over the inviter's, unlike the former instance. It is the refusal to bear this asymmetric relationship in mind which, I believe, has led to much misguided thought concerning God's responsibility in the origin of sin, especially the doctrine of double predestination, which ignores the truth of the second instance here, and the doctrine of works righteousness, which ignores the truth of the first one.

16. In traditional terms, it is true both before and after the Fall.

17. This wording is supplied by Kenneth S. Kantzer, "Unity and Diversity in Evangelical Faith," in David F. Wells and John D. Woodbridge, eds., *The Evangelicals* (Nashville: Abingdon, 1975), p. 38.

18. Thus, the counterpart to the formal principle of Protestantism, the centrality of the Bible, is its material principle which states that "God's loving favor is entered into through faith in Jesus Christ." Kantzer, ibid.

19. This is a theological or conceptual analysis. It will be buttressed with a parallel historical argument when we consider Donatism below.

20. This is not to say that it has not interested evangelicals. A recent treatment may be found in Ronald H. Nashs's *The Word of God and the Mind of Man: The Crisis of Revealed Truth in Contemporary Theology* (Grand Rapids: Zondervan, 1982).

21. This is the "principle of sacramentality" of Catholicism as enunciated by Richard P. McBrien in *Catholicism* (Minneapolis: Winston, 1981), p. 1255. There are two reasons why I feel no hesitation in affirmatively quoting Catholic sources in this study, a practice which is admittedly rare among evangelicals. The narrow reason is that McBrien does not claim that this principle is uniquely Catholic, but only that it is characteristically so; it is the convergence or constellation of three separate principles (sacramentality, mediation, and communion) which conceptually specifies Catholicism in his view (pp. 1180–84). The broad reason draws upon the very principle of sacramentality itself, which is simply another way of stating the effect of the doctrine of creation: in principle, there is no part of God's creation in which truth cannot be found and appreciated. If this is true in general, then it is particularly true of other denominations within the Christian church, even that one against which "Protestants" have traditionally tended to define themselves. While it is surely naïve to think that "Protestant" will recede from general usage, it is equally naïve to believe that all Protestants are protesting Catholicism at the core of their religious lives. In any event, I do not intend the word as a negative self-designation. Nor, to return to the point at hand, can there by any theological justification for restricting ourselves from an avenue through which we may come to know more about God.

22. I mean "operation" here in its broadest possible sense, since, as we will see, one of these moments is largely passive in nature.

23. This is the specific distinction between inspiration and conversion. In conversion the mind suspends and often rejects the normativeness of its prehistory and reformulates an entire new horizon within which it will operate, whereas in inspiration "old" data are illuminated and seen in a new light.

24. Hans Frei's *The Eclipse of Biblical Narrative* (New Haven: Yale University Press, 1974–77) chronicles precisely this confusion among Protestant theologians in the eighteenth and nineteenth centuries.

25. That is, it is irrelevant except for purely literary and historical purposes, purposes which would be dominant in a class on Shakespeare, for example.

26. This is an implication of the moment of transition, since implicit in that voluntary restriction is the possibility of being changed. Since under normal conditions neither the author nor anybody else coerces the reader into accepting the book's message, it is here provisionally accepted *as though* it were the reader's own.

27. Again, we are not here considering conversion, where the entire horizon of expectations itself is altered.

28. This calls to mind the "metaphysics of light" which has proved to be such a powerful metaphor for understanding the coactivity of God in human mental operations. Briefly, the metaphor develops the idea that although light does not cause objects to pass into and out of actual existence, its presence is required if we are to be able to see those objects. Analogously, then, God is said to be light in that His "illumination" is required if we are to be able to see things as they really are, as created by Him and thus capable of mediating His presence. For a treatment of Augustine's exploration of this metaphor, see Ronald H. Nash, *The Light of the Mind: St. Augustine's Theory of Knowledge* (Lexington: University Press of Kentucky, 1969). For similar treatises on Thomas, see Bernard Lonergan, *Verbum: Word and Idea in Aquinas*, ed. by David Burrell (Notre Dame: University of Notre Dame Press, 1967), esp. part II; and Victor Preller, *Divine Science and the Science of God: A Reformulation of Thomas Aquinas* (Princeton: Princeton University Press, 1967), esp. chap. 4.

29. This assertion might initially appear to be a non sequitur. The section on verbal inspiration below, and the final chapter, will attempt to say why it is not.

Chapter 4

1. This analytic component of inspiration will prove to be important in the discussion of inerrancy below.

2. There are technical differences among foundationalism, naïve inductivism, and Scottish realism, but they are members of the same epistemological family.

3. I do not claim, however, that it was obvious to persons in the past, whether evangelicals or not.

4. As Abraham reminds us, inspiration may involve more than this simplified structure, but it involves at least this structure.

5. The reader is reminded that the methodology of this study insists that theory is unable to inform present and future experience until it (in principle) accurately reflects past experience.

6. I have already given one answer to this question in the section on the activity

of the mind; there I said that a text was received as divinely inspired if it contributed to one's own understanding of God as well as to one's own self-understanding. In what follows, I shall consider a second type of response. It is inspired by Bernard Lonergan.

7. They are the scientific, the religious, the scholarly, the modern philosophic, and the aesthetic. Added to the thirty-two combinations available from these types is the undifferentiated consciousness, according to whose outlook only immediate experiences are real. For the rest, though, all experience is mediated experience; the types and combinations of differentiated consciousness are themselves the grids or standards which serve to mediate one's experience of the world in ways which make it a knowable and known world for that person or group. For Lonergan's full treatment of differentiated and undifferentiated consciousness, see *Method in Theology* (New York: Seabury, 1979), esp. chap. 12. A more succinct presentation is found in *Doctrinal Pluralism* (Milwaukee: Marquette University Press, 1971), his 1971 Pere Marquette Theology Lecture.

8. I am not interested here in evaluating the specifics of Lonergan's scheme. I refer to it because of its usefulness in pointing out what I take to be a correct analysis of the history of human consciousness, that the existence of a pluralism of mental outlooks concerning the meaning of experience necessitates in principle a pluralism of theological reflections upon concrete experiences of salvation.

9. There are, of course, many titles used of Jesus in the New Testament. I confine this discussion to Messiah and Son of God.

10. See James Dunn, *Unity and Diversity in the New Testament* (Philadelphia: Westminster, 1977), pp. 41–45.

11. For a similar treatment, see Edward Schillebeeckx, *Jesus* (New York: Crossroad, 1981), esp. pp. 439–515. An earlier work which sees the titles used for Jesus in nonontological ways is Oscar Cullman's *The Christology of the New Testament* (Philadelphia: Westminster, 1963). Unlike Dunn and Schillebeeckx, however, who see the titles as indications of the faith(s) of the communities which used them, Cullmann sees them as indications of the various functions of Jesus. Thus, his work is still primarily interested in Jesus who functioned in various ways rather than in the communities which responded to Jesus in various ways.

12. See Chapter 3, note 5, above.

13. Lindsell uses "infallibility" and "inerrancy" synonymously.

14. Harold Lindsell, *The Battle for the Bible* (Grand Rapids: Zondervan, 1976), pp. 30–31.

15. See also the statement of Edward J. Young of the Old Testament faculty at Westminster Theological Seminary in Philadelphia: "The Bible, according to its own claim, is breathed forth from God. To maintain that there are flaws or errors in it is the same as declaring that there are flaws or errors in God Himself." *Thy Word Is Truth* (Grand Rapids: Eerdmans, 1957), p. 123.

16. Here the reader will recall the discussion above concerning "Messiah" and "Son of God" and the different groups of Christians for whom they constituted the more appropriate expressions of belief in God.

17. Charles M. Wood makes much the same point in his very helpful work *The Formation of Christian Understanding* (Philadelphia: Westminster, 1981), when he

says on p. 102 that "authority is a functional term. Authority is always ultimately derived from and exercised in obedience to an 'authorizer' which is itself not an authority, but rather a *source* of authority. In this sense, the authority of scripture can be properly and fully acknowledged only when it is understood that scripture is not to be confused with that norm [Jesus Christ] which it is authorized to disclose." The reader will also note the conceptual similarity between this understanding of authority and my understanding of inspiration.

18. See James Barr, *Fundamentalism* (Philadelphia: Westminster, 1977–78), pp. 279–84.

19. For a similar treatment, see Stephen T. Davis, *The Debate about the Bible* (Philadelphia: Westminster, 1977), pp. 77–82.

20. Peter Brown, *Augustine of Hippo* (Berkeley and Los Angeles: University of California Press, 1967), p. 215.

21. See Geoffrey Grimshaw Willis, *Saint Augustine and the Donatist Controversy* (London: S.P.C.K., 1950), pp. 1–5, for a discussion of rigorism and liberalism as the two poles between which the church has constantly oscillated in its struggle to deal with the non-Christian society.

22. There are other ways of interpreting Donatism, notably W. H. C. Frend's socioeconomic analysis in *The Donatist Church* (Oxford: Clarendon Press, 1952), esp. pp. 229–38. Frend presents and defends the thesis that Donatism was a rebellion of populist rural believers against Roman-educated (and thus more urbane) bishops. Brown responds to this interpretation in "Religious Dissent in the Later Roman Empire: The Case of North Africa," *History* 46 (1961): 83–101.

23. See Willis, *Saint Augustine*, pp. 8–23.

24. Ibid., p. 144.

25. Ibid., pp. 108–10, 176–77.

26. Cyprian, *Epistulae* LXXII–LXXIV, in *Patrologiae cursus completus, Series Latinus*, ed. by J. P. Migne, cited by Willis in ibid., p. 150.

27. Willis, *Saint Augustine*, p. 145.

28. See Edward Schillebeeckx, *Ministry* (New York: Crossroad, 1981), part I.

29. If there is any usefulness at all to the notion of inerrancy within Christian theology, it is as a statement of belief that the church will be so guided by the Holy Spirit that it will never conclusively err or wander from the gospel as it moves from age to age. That is, even in the worst of times there will always be "seven thousand in Israel who have not bowed the knee to Baal" (II Kings 19:18). This is, however, a doctrine concerning ecclesiology rather than Scripture, and it leaves intact the assertion that inerrancy has no bearing whatever upon the doctrine of Scripture.

Chapter 5

1. For those who wish to explore Rahner's thought in greater depth, the best place to begin is his *Foundations of Christian Thought: An Introduction to the Idea of Christianity* (New York: Seabury, 1978). Three very helpful secondary works on Rahner are Karl-Heinz Weger, *Karl Rahner: An Introduction to His Theology* (New York: Seabury, 1980); Leo O'Donovan, ed., *A World of Grace: An Introduction to the Themes and Foundations of Karl Rahner's Theology* (New York: Seabury, 1980);

and Robert Kress, *A Rahner Handbook* (Atlanta: John Knox, 1982). Gerald McCool has edited a large collection of Rahneria in his *A Rahner Reader* (New York: Seabury, 1975).

2. See above, Chapter 1, pp. 30 ff., and Chapter 4, pp. 89–90.

3. For example, "John's experience of an elephant" has to do both with entities in the world which are external to John and with the interior encounter of those entities by John. Here, it is clear that there is no experience unless both interior and exterior referents are considered.

4. This is the difference between a question and a rhetorical question. The latter does not represent a real expression of finitude, because the answer is completely known to the questioner before asking it. I am not here denying the truth of the maxim "All questions contain the seeds of their answers." When I say that a genuine question opens the questioner to an answer from anywhere, I do not mean to imply that the answer to the sum of "two plus two" could be "cats." I will address this issue in more detail shortly, but for the moment it should be recalled that we are here talking about the universal phenomenon of questioning and not about one specific question within a restricted field of knowledge. If humans may generally be characterized as questioning beings, then they may equally be characterized as beings who are "open to the universe."

5. Since some questions have many answers, we can be more precise here in saying that the set of answers is smaller than the set of possible responses. Thus, the problem of criteria for, or discrimination among, the latter set still exists. For the sake of simplicity, I shall confine the discussion to a single-answer question.

6. It might be objected at this point that I am confusing the categories of "good" and "true" in this account, since typically the criterion for answering questions is truth rather than goodness. I would reply that this is not a category confusion at all, because goodness is a more fundamental category than truth. For example, when an answer to a question is seen to be true, it is legitimate to ask, "But why should I accept this truth and act upon it?" The answer to this question, then, is that the truth should be accepted because it is good. Beyond this, however, one cannot question any further; to ask, "But why should I accept and act upon the good?" is to show one's contempt, or at least cynicism, with respect to human morality. Implicit in an answer's being called true is its being called true because it is good, and goodness is thus seen as more basic or fundamental than truth. Another way to make the same point is to note that while our understanding of truth can and does change, what does not change is the reason why we call anything true: something is true always and only because of its greater contextual goodness.

7. The sole exception seems to be the case of insanity, when by definition all notions of criteria are suspended.

8. An interesting perspective is opened if we choose to translate the Greek words for "except" (*ei me*) literally rather than idiomatically; the verse would then read "No one is good if the one God is not good."

9. See the discussion by David Burrell of Thomas' understanding of goodness in *Exercises in Religious Understanding* (Notre Dame: University of Notre Dame Press, 1974), pp. 106–13.

10. Rahner, *Foundations*, p. 89.

11. Ibid., p. 86.

12. *Theological Dictionary of the New Testament: "eirene"* (II, 400–20) and "*sozo* etc." (VII, 965–1024).

13. This is but another way to refer to Scripture as *norma normans non normata*. In addition, it is the answer to the question asked above about how to distinguish the inspiration of the Bible from that of other books. With extremely rare exceptions, all nonbiblical books written by Christians are reflections upon biblical notions and have thus been inspired by the Bible. Exceptions would be books such as *Didache*, which many take to have been written before the latest canonical works.

14. Here I have in mind, for example, 2 Peter or Jude on the one hand and Augustine's *City of God*, Thomas's *Summa Theologiae*, or Calvin's *Institutes of the Christian Religion* on the other. It may be seen that this is another way to address the Reformation debate between "Scripture and Tradition." Unlike Protestantism, Catholicism saw rightly that Scripture is itself a product of Christian tradition and thus that no material line of demarcation could be drawn between them. However, Catholicism ignored the foundational or chronologically restricted nature of Scripture in its polemic against the Protestants and thus was rightly accused by the latter of having no real Scripture at all. Once the definition of Scripture is seen to include both normative and foundational components, both of the previous shortcomings are overcome, and the way is open for the historical origins of the Bible to be maintained alongside its status as singularly or uniquely authoritative in the church. See D. E. W. Harrison's "The Situation Today," in F. W. Dillistone, ed., *Scripture and Tradition* (London: Lutterworth, 1955), pp. 133–50.

15. See James Dunn, *Unity and Diversity in the New Testament* (Philadelphia: Westminster, 1977), p. 81. In his review of Paul Achtemeier's *The Inspiration of Scripture: Problems and Proposals* (Philadelphia: Westminster, 1980), Francis Schüssler Fiorenza makes the same point. Using the term "transformative" to refer to what I have called the normative aspect of Scripture, he asked rhetorically: "Does Achtemeier's emphasis upon the transformative power of the content . . . sufficiently ground inspiration? It does if one understands that because of the transformative power of the texts they came to have a foundational and constitutive significance for the Christian community. It does not if this transformative power is understood in isolation from this foundational significance." *Catholic Biblical Quarterly* 43 (1981): 635–37.

16. Hans von Campenhausen, *The Formation of the Christian Bible* (Philadelphia: Fortress, 1979), p. x.

17. Ibid., pp. 222–23.

18. Karl Rahner, *Inspiration in the Bible* (New York: Herder and Herder, 1962), pp. 55–80.

19. See David Kelsey, *The Uses of Scripture in Recent Theology* (Philadelphia: Fortress, 1975), p. 93.

20. Thus, my specific criticism of Kelsey is that he is vague concerning foundationality, much as Fiorenza noticed with respect to Achtemeier; see above, note 15.

Bibliography

Abba, Raymond. *The Nature and Authority of the Bible*. London: James Clarke, 1958.

Abraham, William J. *The Divine Inspiration of Holy Scripture*. Oxford: Oxford University Press, 1981.

————. *Divine Revelation and the Limits of Historical Criticism*. Oxford: Oxford University Press, 1982.

Achtemeier, Paul. *The Inspiration of Scripture: Problems and Proposals*. Philadelphia: Westminster, 1980.

Ahlstrom, Sidney. "The Scottish Philosophy and American Theology." *Church History* 24 (1955): 257–72.

Barr, James. *The Bible in the Modern World*. New York: Harper and Row, 1973.

————. *Fundamentalism*. London: SCM, 1977.

————. *Old and New in Interpretation*. London: SCM, 1966.

Beegle, Dewey M. *The Inspiration of Scripture*. Philadelphia: Westminster, 1963.

————. *Scripture, Tradition, and Infallibility*. Grand Rapids: Eerdmans, 1973.

Benoit, P. *Aspects of Inspiration*. Chicago: Priory, 1965.

Berkhof, Louis. *Systematic Theology*. Grand Rapids: Eerdmans, 1946.

Berkouwer, G. C. *General Revelation*. Grand Rapids: Eerdmans, 1955.

————. *Holy Scripture*, trans. by Jack Rogers. Grand Rapids: Eerdmans, 1975.

Blanshard, Brand. *Reason and Analysis*. LaSalle, Ill.: Open Court, 1973.

Bloesch, Donald. *Essentials of Evangelical Theology*, vol. 2, *Life, Ministry and Hope*. San Francisco: Harper and Row, 1979.

————. *The Evangelical Renaissance*. Grand Rapids: Eerdmans, 1973.

Boice, James M. *The Foundations of Biblical Authority*. Grand Rapids: Zondervan, 1978.

Bright, John. *The Authority of the Old Testament*. Nashville: Abingdon, 1967.

Brown, Peter. *Augustine of Hippo*. Berkeley: University of California Press, 1967.

Brown, Raymond E. *Biblical Reflections on Crises Facing the Church*. New York: Paulist, 1975.

Burnaby, John. *Is The Bible Inspired?* London: Duckworth, 1949.

Burrell, David. *Exercises in Religious Understanding.* Notre Dame: University of Notre Dame Press, 1974.

Burtchaell, James T. *Catholic Theories of Biblical Inspiration since 1810: A Review and Critique.* Cambridge: Cambridge University Press, 1969.

Bush, L. Russ, and Tom J. Nettles. *Baptists and the Bible.* Chicago: Moody, 1980.

Buswell, James Oliver, Jr. *A Christian View of Being and Knowing.* Grand Rapids: Zondervan, 1960.

Carnell, Edward John. *The Case for Biblical Christianity*, ed. by Ronald H. Nash. Grand Rapids: Eerdmans, 1969.

————. *The Case for Orthodox Theology.* Philadelphia: Westminster, 1959.

————. *Christian Commitment.* New York: Macmillan, 1957.

————. *An Introduction to Christian Apologetics.* Grand Rapids: Eerdmans, 1950.

Carpenter, Joel A. "Fundamentalist Institutions and the Rise of Evangelical Protestantism, 1929–1942." *Church History* 49 (March 1980): 62–75.

Carson, D. A., and John Woodbridge, eds. *Scripture and Truth.* Grand Rapids: Zondervan, 1981.

————. *A Christian View of Men and Things.* Grand Rapids: Eerdmans, 1952–60.

Clark, Gordon H. *A Christian Philosophy of Education.* Grand Rapids: Eerdmans, 1946.

————. *Religion, Reason and Revelation.* Nutley, N.J.: Presbyterian and Reformed, 1961.

Coats, G. W., and B. O. Long, eds. *Canon and Authority.* Philadelphia: Fortress, 1977.

Costello, Charles J. *St. Augustine's Doctrine of the Inspiration and Canonicity of Scripture.* Washington: Catholic University of America, 1930.

Cullmann, Oscar. *The Christology of the New Testament.* Philadelphia: Westminster, 1963.

Cunliffe-Jones, Hubert. *The Authority of the Biblical Revelation.* London: Clarke, 1945.

Davis, Stephen T. *The Debate about the Bible.* Philadelphia: Westminster, 1977.

Dayton, Donald W. *Discovering an Evangelical Heritage.* New York: Harper and Row, 1976.

Diamond, Malcolm, and Thomas Litzenburg, Jr., eds. *The Logic of God: Theology and Verification.* Indianapolis: Bobbs-Merrill, 1975.

Dillistone, F. W., ed. *Scripture and Tradition.* London: Lutterworth, 1955.

Dodd, C. H. *The Authority of the Bible.* London: Nisbet, 1929.

Dulles, Avery. "The Bible in the Church: Some Debated Questions." In G. Martin, ed., *Scripture and the Charismatic Renewal.* Ann Arbor: Servant, 1979.

Dunn, James D. G. *Unity and Diversity in the New Testament: An Inquiry into the Character of Earliest Christianity.* Philadelphia: Westminster, 1977.

Erickson, Millard. *The New Evangelical Theology.* London: Marshall, Morgan and Scott, 1969.

Evans, Donald. *The Logic of Self-Involvement.* London: SCM, 1963.

Fortescue, Adrian. *Donatism*. London: Burns & Oates, 1917.

Frei, Hans. *The Eclipse of Biblical Narrative*. New Haven: Yale University Press, 1974–77.

Frend, W. H. C. *The Donatist Church*. Oxford: Clarendon Press, 1952.

Gaspar, Louis. *The Fundamentalist Movement*. The Hague: Mouton, 1963.

Gaussen, Louis. *The Inspiration of the Holy Scriptures*, trans. by David D. Scott. Chicago: Moody, 1949.

Geisler, Norman, ed. *Inerrancy*. Grand Rapids: Zondervan, 1979.

———. *Philosophy of Religion*. Grand Rapids: Zondervan, 1974.

Gerstner, John H. *A Bible Inerrancy Primer*. Grand Rapids: Baker, 1965.

———. *Reasons for Faith*. New York: Harper and Brothers, 1960.

Gill, Jerry H. *The Possibility of Religious Language*. Grand Rapids: Eerdmans, 1971.

Harris, R. Laird. *Inspiration and Canonicity of the Bible*. Grand Rapids: Zondervan, 1957.

Hatch, Nathan, and Mark Noll, eds. *The Bible in America*. New York: Oxford University Press, 1982.

Henry, Carl F. H. *The Case for Orthodox Theology*. Philadelphia: Westminster, 1959.

———. *Evangelicals in Search of Identity*. Waco, Tex.: Word, 1976.

———. *God, Revelation and Authority*, Vol. I, *God Who Speaks and Shows*. Waco, Tex.: Word, 1976.

———. *The God Who Shows Himself*. Waco, Tex.: Word, 1966.

———. *Notes on the Doctrine of God*. Boston: Wilde, 1948.

———. *Personal Idealism and Strong's Theology*. Wheaton, Ill.: Van Kampen, 1951.

———. *The Protestant Dilemma*. Grand Rapids: Eerdmans, 1949.

———. *Revelation and the Bible*. Grand Rapids: Eerdmans, 1958.

———. *The Uneasy Conscience of Modern Fundamentalism*. Grand Rapids: Eerdmans, 1947.

Hodge, Archibald A. *The Life of Charles Hodge*. New York: Arno and the *New York Times*, 1969.

Hodge, Archibald A., and Benjamin B. Warfield. *Inspiration*. Grand Rapids: Baker, 1979.

Hodge, Charles. *Systematic Theology*. New York: Scribner, 1871.

Hoffman, Thomas J. "Inspiration, Normativeness, Canonicity, and the Unique Sacred Character of the Bible." *Catholic Biblical Quarterly* 44 (July 1982): 447–69.

Hooykas, R. *Religion and the Rise of Modern Science*. Grand Rapids: Eerdmans, 1978.

Hutcheson, Richard G., Jr. *Mainline Churches and the Evangelicals: A Challenging Crisis?* Atlanta: Knox, 1981.

Inch, Morris. *The Evangelical Challenge*. Philadelphia: Westminster, 1978.

Johnston, Robert K. *Evangelicals at an Impasse: Biblical Authority in Practice*. Atlanta: Knox, 1979.

Kelly, J. N. D. *Early Christian Doctrines*. New York: Harper and Row, 1958–60.

Kelsey, David H. *The Uses of Scripture in Recent Theology*. London: SCM, 1975.

Kress, Robert. *A Rahner Handbook*. Atlanta: John Knox, 1982.

Küng, Hans, and Jürgen Moltmann. *Conflicting Ways of Interpreting the Bible*. Edinburgh: Clark, and New York: Seabury, 1980.

Ladd, George Eldon. *The Blessed Hope*. Grand Rapids: Eerdmans, 1956.

―――. *The New Testament and Criticism*. Grand Rapids: Eerdmans, 1967.

―――. *The Pattern of New Testament Truth*. Grand Rapids: Eerdmans, 1968.

Leith, John, ed. *Creeds of the Church*. Richmond: John Knox, 1963.

Levie, Jean. *The Bible, The Word of God in Words of Men*. New York: Kennedy & Sons, 1961–64.

Lewis, Edwin C. *A Philosophy of the Christian Revelation*. New York: Harper and Brothers, 1940.

Lindsell, Harold. *The Battle for the Bible*. Grand Rapids: Zondervan, 1976.

Lonergan, Bernard. *Doctrinal Pluralism*. Marquette: Marquette University Press, 1971.

―――. *Method in Theology*. New York: Seabury, 1979.

―――. *Verbum: Word and Idea in Aquinas*, ed. by David Burrell. Notre Dame: University of Notre Dame Press, 1967.

McBrien, Richard P. *Catholicism*. Minneapolis: Winston, 1981.

McClendon, James, and James Smith. *Understanding Religious Convictions*. Notre Dame: University of Notre Dame Press, 1975.

McCool, Gerald. *A Rahner Reader*. New York: Seabury, 1975.

McDonald, H. O. *Theories of Revelation: An Historical Study, 1700–1960*. Grand Rapids: Baker, 1979.

McKenzie, J. L. "The Social Character of Inspiration." *Catholic Biblical Quarterly* 24 (1962): 115–24.

McLoughlin, William, ed. *The American Evangelicals 1800–1900*. New York: Harper and Row, 1968.

Marshall, I. Howard. *Biblical Inspiration*. Grand Rapids: Eerdmans, 1982.

Marxsen, Willi. *The Resurrection of Jesus of Nazareth*. Philadelphia: Westminster, 1979.

Mavrodes, George. *Fundamentalists and American Culture*. New York: Oxford University Press, 1980.

Mitchell, Basil. *The Justification of Religious Belief*. London: Macmillan, 1973.

Montgomery, John W., ed. *God's Inerrant Word*. Minneapolis: Bethany, 1974.

―――. *The Shape of the Past: An Introduction to Philosophical Historiography*. Ann Arbor: Edwards Brothers, 1963.

―――. *The Suicide of Christian Theology*. Minneapolis: Bethany, 1971.

Nash, Ronald H. *The Light of the Mind: St. Augustine's Theory of Knowledge*. Lexington: University of Kentucky Press, 1969.

―――. *The New Evangelicalism*. Grand Rapids: Zondervan, 1963.

―――, ed. *The Philosophy of Gordon Clark: A Festschrift*. Philadelphia: Presbyterian and Reformed, 1968.

―――. *The Word of God and the Mind of Man: The Crisis of Revealed Truth in Contemporary Theology*. Grand Rapids: Zondervan, 1982.

Nelson, Rudolph L. "Fundamentalism at Harvard: The Case of Edward John Carnell." *Quarterly Review* 2 (Summer 1982): 79–98.

Newman, John Henry. *An Essay in Aid of a Grammar of Assent*. Notre Dame: University of Notre Dame Press, 1979.

O'Donovan, Leo, ed. *A World of Grace: An Introduction to the Themes and Foundations of Karl Rahner's Theology*. New York: Seabury, 1980.

Orr, James. *The Christian View of God and the World*. Grand Rapids: Eerdmans, 1947.

———. *Revelation and Inspiration*. Grand Rapids: Eerdmans, 1952.

Packer, James I. *"Fundamentalism" and the Word of God*. London: Inter-Varsity, 1958.

———. *God Speaks to Man: Revelation and the Bible*. Philadelphia: Westminster, 1965.

Padilla, Rene C., ed. *The New Face of Evangelicalism*. Urbana, Ill.: InterVarsity, 1976.

Pieper, Franz. *Christian Dogmatics*. St. Louis: Concordia, 1950.

Pinnock, Clark. *A Defense of Biblical Inerrancy*. Nutley, N.J.: Presbyterian and Reformed, 1967.

Plantinga, Alvin. "The Reformed Objection to Natural Theology." *Christian Scholar's Review* 11 (1982): 187–98.

Preller, Victor. *Divine Science and the Science of God: A Reformulation of Thomas Aquinas*. Princeton: Princeton University Press, 1967.

Quebedeaux, Richard. *The Worldly Evangelicals*. New York: Harper and Row, 1978.

———. *The Young Evangelicals*. New York: Harper and Row, 1974.

Rahner, Karl. *Foundations of Christian Thought: An Introduction to the Idea of Christianity*. New York: Seabury, 1978.

———. *Inspiration in the Bible*. New York: Herder and Herder, 1961.

Ramm, Bernard. *After Fundamentalism: The Future of Evangelical Theology*. San Francisco: Harper and Row, 1982.

———. *The Christian View of Science and Scripture*. Grand Rapids: Eerdmans, 1955.

———. *The Devil, Seven Wormwoods, and God*. Waco, Tex.: Word, 1977.

———. *The Evangelical Heritage*. Waco, Tex.: Word, 1973.

———. *The God Who Makes a Difference: A Christian Appeal to Reason*. Waco, Tex.: Word, 1972.

———. *A Handbook of Contemporary Theology*. Grand Rapids: Eerdmans, 1966.

———. *The Pattern of Religious Authority*. Grand Rapids, Eerdmans, 1959.

———. *Protestant Biblical Interpretation*. Grand Rapids: Baker, 1970.

———. *Special Revelation and the Word of God*. Grand Rapids: Eerdmans, 1961.

———. *Types of Apologetic Systems*. Wheaton, Ill.: Van Kampen, 1953.

———. *The Witness of the Spirit*. Grand Rapids: Eerdmans, 1959.

Ramsey, Ian T. *Models and Mystery*. London: Oxford University Press, 1964.

———. *Religious Language: An Empirical Placing of Theological Phrases*. London: SCM, 1963.

Reid, J. K. S. *The Authority of Scripture*. New York: Harper, 1957.

Reid, Thomas. *Philosophical Works*. Hildesheim: Georg Olms Verlagsbuchhandlung, 1967.

Reumann, John, Samuel H. Nafzger, and Harold H. Ditmanson, eds. *Studies in Lutheran Hermeneutics*. Philadelphia: Fortress, 1979.

Richardson, Alan, and W. Schweitzer, eds. *Biblical Authority for Today*. London: SCM, 1951.

Ricoeur, Paul. *Essays on Biblical Interpretation*, ed. by Lewis S. Mudge. Philadelphia: Fortress, 1980.

Ridderbos, Herman. *Studies in Scripture and Its Authority*. St. Catherines, Ont.: Paideia, 1978.

Rogers, Jack, ed. *Biblical Authority*. Waco, Tex.: Word, 1977.

———. *Confessions of a Conservative Evangelical*. Philadelphia: Westminster, 1974.

Rogers, Jack, and Donald McKim. *The Authority and Interpretation of the Bible*. San Francisco: Harper and Row, 1979.

Sanday, William. *Inspiration*. London: Green, 1903.

———. *The Oracles of God*. London: Longmans, Green, 1892.

Sandeen, Ernest R. *The Origins of Fundamentalism*. Philadelphia: Fortress, 1968.

———. *The Roots of Fundamentalism: British and American Millenarianism 1800–1930*. Chicago: University of Chicago Press, 1970.

Schaeffer, Francis. *Escape from Reason*. Downers Grove, Ill.: Inter-Varsity, 1968.

———. *The God Who Is There*. Downers Grove, Ill.: Inter-Varsity, 1968.

———. *No Final Conflict: The Bible without Error in All That It Affirms*. Downers Grove, Ill.: Inter-Varsity, 1975.

———. *Two Contents, Two Realities*. Downers Grove, Ill.: Inter-Varsity, 1974.

Schillebeeckx, Edward. *Jesus*. New York: Crossroad, 1981.

———. *Ministry*. New York: Crossroad, 1981.

Schökel, L. Alonso. *The Inspired Word: Scripture in the Light of Language and Literature*. New York: Herder and Herder, 1965.

Scullion, J. *The Theology of Inspiration*. Notre Dame: Fides, 1970.

Shelley, Bruce L. *Evangelicalism in America*. Grand Rapids: Eerdmans, 1967.

Sheppard, Gerald T. "Biblical Hermeneutics: The Academic Language of Evangelical Identity." *Union Seminary Quarterly Review* 32 (Winter 1977): 81–94.

———. "Recovering the Natural Sense." *Theology Today* 38 (1981): 330–37.

Smart, James D. *The Interpretation of Scripture*. Philadelphia: Westminster, 1961.

———. *The Strange Silence of the Bible in the Church*. Philadelphia: Westminster, 1970.

Smith, Timothy. *Revivalism and Social Reform in Mid-Nineteenth-Century America*. New York: Abingdon, 1957.

Smyth, John Patterson. *The Bible in the Making in the Light of Modern Research*. New York: James Pott, 1914.

———. *How God Inspired the Bible*. New York: James Pott, 1893.

———. *How We Got Our Bible*. New York: James Pott, 1926.

Snaith, Norman H. *The Inspiration and Authority of the Bible*. London: Epworth, 1956.

Stearns, Lewis French. *Evidence of Christian Experience*. London: Nisbet, 1890.

Stibbs, Alan. *Understanding God's Word*. London: Inter-Varsity, 1962.

Stott, John R. W. *Understanding the Bible*. Glendale, Calif.: Regal, 1972.

Strong, Augustus H. *Christ in Creation and Ethical Monism*. Philadelphia: Griffith and Rowland, 1899.

———. *Philosophy and Religion*. New York: A. C. Armstrong and Son, 1888.

———. *Systematic Theology*. Valley Forge, Pa.: Judson, 1907.

Stuhlmacher, Peter. *Historical Criticism and Theological Interpretation of Scripture*, trans. by Roy A. Harrisville. Philadelphia: Fortress, 1977.

Sundberg, A. C. "The Bible Canon and the Christian Doctrine of Inspiration." *Interpretation* 29 (1975): 364–71.

Surburg, Raymond F. *How Dependable is the Bible?* Philadelphia and New York: J. Lippencott, 1972.

Taylor, Vincent. "Religious Certainty." *The Expository Times* 72 (November 60): 15–18, 49–52.

Thiessen, Henry C. *Introductory Lectures in Systematic Theology*. Grand Rapids: Eerdmans, 1949.

Thiselton, Anthony C. *The Two Horizons: New Testament Hermeneutics and Philosophical Description*. Grand Rapids: Eerdmans, 1980.

Tilley, Terrence W. *Talking of God*. New York: Paulist, 1978.

Tillich, Paul. *Systematic Theology*. Chicago: University of Chicago Press, 1951.

Torrance, Thomas F. *Reality and Evangelical Theology*. Philadelphia: Westminster, 1982.

Van der Leeuw, Gerhardus. *Creeds of the Church*. Richmond: John Knox, 1963.

Van Til, Cornelius. *A Christian Theory of Knowledge*. Philadelphia: Presbyterian and Reformed, 1975.

———. *The Defense of the Faith*. Philadelphia: Presbyterian and Reformed, 1955.

———. *The Doctrine of Scripture*. Ripon, Calif.: Den Dulk, 1967.

———. *An Introduction to Systematic Theology*. Philadelphia: Presbyterian and Reformed, 1974.

Vawter, Bruce. *Biblical Inspiration*. London: Hutchinson, and Philadelphia: Westminster, 1972.

Von Campenhausen, Hans. *The Formation of the Christian Bible*, trans. by J. A. Baker. Philadelphia: Fortress, 1972.

Walvoord, John E., ed. *Inspiration and Inerrancy*. Grand Rapids: Eerdmans, 1957.

Warfield, Benjamin B. *Biblical and Theological Studies*, ed. by Samuel G. Craig. Nutley, N.J.: Presbyterian and Reformed, 1952.

———. *The Inspiration and Authority of the Bible*. Philadelphia: Presbyterian and Reformed, 1948.

———. *Introduction to the Textual Criticism of the New Testament*. London: Hodder and Stoughton, 1886.

———. *Revelation and Inspiration*. New York: Oxford University Press, 1927.

———. *Studies in Apologetics*. New York: Oxford University Press, 1932.

———. *The Westminster Assembly and Its Work*. Cherry Hill, N.J.: Mack, 1972.

Webber, Robert, and Donald Bloesch, eds. *The Orthodox Evangelicals*. Nashville and New York: Thomas Nelson, 1978.

Weger, Karl-Heinz. *Karl Rahner: An Introduction to His Theology*. New York: Seabury, 1980.

Wells, David F., and John Woodbridge. *The Evangelicals*. Nashville and New York: Abingdon, 1975.

Wenger, J. C. *God's Written Word*. Scottdale, Pa.: Herald Press, 1966.

Wenham, John. *Christ and the Bible*. London: InterVarsity, 1972.

Willis, Geoffrey Grimshaw. *Saint Augustine and the Donatist Controversy*. London: S.P.C.K., 1950.

Wood, Charles M. *The Formation of Christian Understanding*. Philadelphia: Westminster, 1981.

Woodbridge, John. "Biblical Authority: Towards an Evaluation of the Rogers and McKim Proposal." *Trinity Journal* ns 1 (1980): 165–236.

———. *Biblical Authority*. Grand Rapids: Zondervan, 1982.

Young, Edward J. *Thy Word Is Truth*. Grand Rapids: Eerdmans, 1957.

Name Index

Abbott, Walter M., 132n
Abraham, William, 8, 64–70, 72, 76, 82, 85, 115
Achtemeier, Paul, 6, 133n, 142n
Ahlstrom, Sidney E., 121n
Aquinas, Thomas, 69, 109, 133n, 134n, 135n, 138n, 141n, 142n
Aristotle, 132n
Augustine, 100–3, 138n, 142n
Ayer, A. J., 35–36, 127n

Barr, James, 130n, 140n
Black, Max, 29, 124n
Blanshard, Brand, 125n, 127n
Brown, Peter, 140n
Brown, Raymond, 135n
Bultmann, Rudolf, 35
Burrell, David, 133n, 134n, 135n, 138n, 141n
Burtchaell, James T., 3, 119n, 136n

Calvin, John, 123n, 142n
Carnell, Edward John, 37–46
Carpenter, Joel, 127n
Clark, Gordon, 37, 129n
Constantine, 100
Cullmann, Oscar, 139n
Cyprian, 101, 140n

Davis, H. Francis, 129n
Davis, Stephen T., 140n
Diamond, Malcolm, 125n

Dillistone, F. W., 142n
Donatus, 100
Dunn, James D. G., 5, 94, 119n, 139n, 142n

Engelland, Hans, 59, 131n
Evans, Donald, 37, 145n

Fiorenza, Francis S., 142n
Frei, Hans, 138n
Frend, W. H. C., 140n

Gerstner, John H., 120n, 122n

Harrison, D. E. W., 142n
Hempel, Carl, 127n
Henry, Carl F. H., 48, 129n, 130n
Heppe, Heinrich, 132n
Hick, John, 33
Hodge, Archibald A., 119n, 121n, 123n
Hodge, Charles, 10–20, 46, 50, 73, 75
Hoffmann, Thomas, 135n
Hooykas, R., 135n

Johnston, Robert K., 119n

Kant, Immanuel, 10, 35, 49
Kantzer, Kenneth, 119n, 137n
Kelsey, David, 117, 121n, 129n, 142n
Kress, Robert, 141n

Leith, John, 120n
Lindsell, Harold, 74, 97, 136n, 139n

Litzenburg, Thomas, Jr., 125n
Lonergan, Bernard, 93, 138n, 139n

Macquarrie, John, 73
Marxsen, Willi, 125n
Mavrodes, George M., 121n
McBrien, Richard P., 137n
McCool, Gerald, 141n
McKim, Donald, 19, 120n, 121n
Mensurius, 100
Montgomery, John Warwick, 27–37, 46, 73

Nash, Ronald, 125n, 129n, 137n, 138n
Nelson, Rudolph L., 127n
Newman, John Henry, 129n
Nicole, Roger, 121n, 122n, 123n
Nielsen, Kai, 125n

O'Donovan, Leo, 141n
Orr, James, 34
Parsons, Mike, 26, 121n, 122n, 123n
Pieper, Francis, 134n
Pierce, C. S., 124n
Plantinga, Alvin, 125n, 129n
Preller, Victor, 138n

Rahner, Karl, 5, 104–9, 114, 140n, 142n
Ramm, Bernard, 57–64
Ramsey, Ian, 30, 33, 124n, 135n
Reid, Thomas, 19, 121n
Rogers, Jack, 19, 120n, 121n

Sanday, William, 131n
Sandeen, Ernest, 20, 121n, 123n, 124n
Schaeffer, Francis, 74, 136n
Schillebeeckx, Edward, 139n, 140n
Schleiermacher, Friedrich, 105
Sheppard, Gerald, 74, 136n
Singer, Peter, 136n
Strong, Augustus H., 48–57
Stuhlmacher, Peter, 130n

Taylor, Vincent, 132n
Thiselton, Anthony, 74, 126n, 127n, 136n
Tilley, Terrence, 126n, 127n, 130n
Tillich, Paul, 125n

Van Til, Cornelius, 38, 119n, 122n
Von Campenhausen, Hans, 112–13, 142n

Warfield, Benjamin B., 6, 20–27, 46, 50–51, 73, 118
Weger, Karl-Heinz, 140n
Wells, David F., 119n, 137n
Willis, Geoffrey Grimshaw, 140n
Wittgenstein, Ludwig, 28, 31, 33, 75, 126n, 133n, 134n
Wood, Charles M., 140n
Woodbridge, John D., 119n, 120n, 123n, 137n

Young, Edward J., 139n

Subject Index

Author, biblical, 13–14, 22, 80–81
Autographs, 17, 24–26, 42–44, 53–54, 99–100

Bible
definition, 6
evaluator of "facts," 11
storehouse of "facts," 10–11, 27, 29, 38
Biblical authority, 18, 22, 31, 43–44, 52–53, 92–93

Canon, 112–14
Certainty
dual sources of, 30–32
religious, 28, 88–90
Concursus, 22–23, 59
Cultural diversity, 93–94

Deductivism, 5, 8–46, 74
Donatism, 97, 100–3
Dualism, 34

Evangelicalism, description, 4–5, 95–96, 104
Existentialism, 35
Experience, 30, 60, 76–77, 90, 99, 105–6

Fundamentalism, 5, 16, 57–58, 96

God and goodness, 107–9

Historical criticism, 9, 16, 18, 42, 59
History as model for theology, 27–37

Image of God, 49, 75–77
Imagination, 29–33
Inductivism, 5, 47–71, 74
Inerrancy, 16–17, 22, 26, 34, 38–39, 43, 48, 52–57, 72, 96–103, 115
Infallibility, 12, 14, 30
Inspiration
biblical, 109–15
and the community, 7, 45–46, 109–14, 117
description, 6–7, 45, 56–58, 67, 104, 109–14
divine, 85–86, 109–14
and divine speaking, 64–68
effects of, 6–7, 47, 50, 55, 62–64, 67, 69, 80, 103, 116
as enhancement, 99, 103, 110–14
as immediate, 8–46
as mediate, 47–71, 87–103, 115–16
plenary, 14, 72, 92–96
teacher as model of, 48, 65–68
verbal, 72, 88–92
Internal witness of the Spirit, 48, 57–64

Language, and knowledge, 19, 41–42, 98–99

Miracles, 55–57
Modern science as model for theology, 9–11, 17, 20, 28–32, 49, 74
Montanism, 113

Operations of the mind, 81–86

Philosophy as model for theology, 28,
    37–45
Prophecy
    as model of inspiration, 13
    as witness to inspiration, 55–57
Providence, 12

Responsibility, 77, 78
Resurrection, 32, 33
Revelation, 13, 21, 30, 50, 58, 67

Salvation, 4, 6, 60, 68, 80–81, 88–91, 103,
    110–14, 116
Scripture, definition, 6
Sin, effects upon mind, 18–19, 21–22, 50,
    59, 75, 77–78

Subjectivism, 30, 34, 89–90, 105–6
Systematic consistency, 9, 38–44

Theological anthropology
    description, 3, 21, 75–81
    inspiration and the mind, 81
Theological methodology, 72–75
Theopneustos, 5–6, 22, 54
Transcendental subjectivism, 105–9
Truthfulness, 8, 28, 31, 35, 38–41, 62–63,
    78

Verification, 30, 35, 39, 73